flowering

advita mundhra

INDIA • SINGAPORE • MALAYSIA

Copyright © Advita Mundhra 2024
All Rights Reserved.

ISBN
Hardcase 979-8-89610-322-6
Paperback 979-8-89588-288-7

This book has been published with all efforts taken to make the material error-free after the consent of the author. However, the author and the publisher do not assume and hereby disclaim any liability to any party for any loss, damage, or disruption caused by errors or omissions, whether such errors or omissions result from negligence, accident, or any other cause.

While every effort has been made to avoid any mistake or omission, this publication is being sold on the condition and understanding that neither the author nor the publishers or printers would be liable in any manner to any person by reason of any mistake or omission in this publication or for any action taken or omitted to be taken or advice rendered or accepted on the basis of this work. For any defect in printing or binding the publishers will be liable only to replace the defective copy by another copy of this work then available.

To those who dare to dream:

you are exactly, precisely and perfectly what you are waiting for.

One day, those dreams sent off into the ocean in their corkscrewed bottles will be answered, and it will be more beautiful than you can ever imagine. So hold on.

"For my part, I know nothing with any certainty, but the sight of the stars makes me dream."

Vincent Van Gogh

contents

foreword   7

preface   9

introduction   13

prologue   15

1. sunrise   19
2. selcouth   23
3. kalopsia   27
4. parasite   35
5. agowilt   41
6. douleur   47
7. rancour   51
8. lacuna   57
9. petrichor   61
10. desvelado   67
11. komorebi   73

contents

12.	apricity	79
13.	sillage	93
14.	cicatrize	99
15.	metanoia	105
16.	koi no yokan	111
17.	querencia	115
18.	raison d'être	121
19.	oubaitori	129
20.	wabi sabi	141

epilogue — *143*
conclusion — *145*
poet's notes — *149*
with gratitude — *163*
author bio — *167*

foreword

Advita's collection of poems *flowering* is entirely what it claims to be – a capturing of the essence of transformation – echoes drawn from moments of transience, wonder, emotion, realisation, metamorphoses and emergence.

The titles of the poems, drawn from multiple languages, infuse the collection with an overarching sense of nuance, adding a sense of shade and subtle refinement to the exploration each individual poem voices. Shifting between the elusive, the exact and the transient, the tonality of the collection varies like the different stages in the process of 'flowering' it seeks to encapsulate.

The lyricism of *flowering*, rich with imagery and metaphorical depth are an ode to simplicity and the beauty of nature; to the unfolding of the self at different paces and in different ways, unhurried and unforced; and to the variations of the human experience inherent in the journey of coming into one's own.

In a world and social context that is far too often driven by the pressure to be a certain way, by a certain time and in a certain manner, it is both refreshing as well as reassuring to go through these poems and experience their resistance to conformity of the singular and the prescribed.

foreword

The poems tell the story of the journey towards selfhood – the dead ends, the crossroads, and the detours; the pain and the pleasure; pinnacles and valleys, pastures and forests, storms and silence, sunsets and the splendour of dawn.

And finally, a sense of celebration and wonder at the singular act of becoming.

By Dr. Sonal Parmar

preface

In the quiet embrace of nature, where the wind whispers ancient secrets and the earth holds stories untold, I found the seed of what would become *flowering*. This collection of poetry is not merely a compilation of words and verses; it is the culmination of a journey—a journey that began in the wild, untamed landscapes of Tasmania and the towering peaks of the Dolomites, but which reached far beyond the physical, delving into the depths of the human spirit.

The concept of *flowering* is rich with meaning, encompassing not only the literal act of blooming but also the metaphorical process of growth, transformation, and becoming. It is a word that speaks to the unfolding of potential, the slow, deliberate emergence of something beautiful and profound from what was once hidden or dormant. This idea resonated deeply with me as I traversed the rugged terrains of the wilderness, where each step forward required a balance between strength and vulnerability, perseverance and surrender.

The inspiration for this collection came during a four-day trek along the jagged cliffs of Tasmania's Bay of Fires. The raw beauty of the landscape, with its turquoise waters and weathered granite shores, stirred something within me that

I had not felt before—a deep, almost primal connection to the world around me. The isolation of the wilderness, coupled with the relentless demands of the trail, stripped away the layers of comfort and familiarity, leaving me face to face with the essence of survival and self-discovery. It was here, amidst the stark contrasts of nature, that I began to mentally pen the first lines of what would become this collection—a testament to growth, healing, and the profound interconnectedness of humanity and the environment.

Each poem in *flowering* is a reflection of the different stages of this journey. The titles themselves—drawn from a tapestry of languages as diverse as the experiences that inspired them—serve as signposts along the way, guiding the reader through the landscapes of emotion, thought, and memory. *komorebi*, a Japanese word describing the interplay of light through the leaves, became a metaphor for the delicate balance between fragility and strength, while *desvelado*, a Spanish word meaning sleepless, echoed the restless nights I spent contemplating the vastness of the world and my place within it. The linguistic diversity of these titles mirrors the multifaceted nature of human experience, each word capturing a nuance, a shade of meaning that might otherwise be lost in translation.

The process of writing these poems was, in many ways, akin to the act of flowering itself—a gradual unfolding, a slow but steady emergence of thoughts and feelings that had long been dormant. There were moments of intense clarity, where the words seemed to flow effortlessly, as if they had been waiting for just the right moment to reveal themselves. But there were also moments of struggle, where the path forward was obscured, and I had to trust in the process, in the idea that the act of creation is often as much about perseverance as it is about inspiration.

This collection is not just a personal exploration of growth and transformation; it is also an invitation to the reader to engage in their own process of flowering. Each poem is a step along the path, a moment in time captured in verse, but also a reflection of the universal experience of becoming. We all bloom in our own time, in our own way, just as the flowers in a meadow do—each one unique, each one contributing to the beauty of the whole.

As you journey through these pages, you will encounter a range of emotions, from the pain of loss and betrayal to the quiet peace of acceptance and the joy of newfound love. You will walk alongside me as I navigate the rough waters of doubt and fear, and you will stand with me in the calm stillness of understanding and resolution. But most importantly, I hope that you will find echoes of your own experiences within these lines, and that *flowering* will serve as a companion on your own journey of growth and transformation.

The act of flowering is not always easy, nor is it always beautiful in the conventional sense. There are thorns and rough patches, moments of darkness and doubt. But it is in these very imperfections that true beauty is found—the beauty of a life lived fully, of a heart opened to the world, of a soul that has embraced both the light and the shadow. This is the essence of *flowering*, and it is my hope that these poems will inspire you to find the beauty in your own process of becoming, in your own unique flowering.

May these words accompany you as you discover the petals of your own story, unfolding with each step and every breath, as you bloom into the person you are meant to be.

introduction

flowering is a meditation on growth, change, and the inevitability of transformation. At its heart, this collection is an exploration of the moments in life when we evolve—sometimes gradually, like the slow unfolding of a petal, and sometimes suddenly, like a tree struck by lightning. Each poem exists within the tension between fragility and strength, pain and healing, loss and renewal.

Nature, in all its cycles, mirrors our own internal landscapes. The poems within these pages draw on that connection, using the elements—earth, air, water, and fire—as metaphors for the emotions and experiences that shape us. From the first rays of sunrise to the lingering scent of rain-soaked earth, these natural phenomena serve as a reflection of the human experience. We grow, much like the flora around us, sometimes in silence, sometimes through storms, but always toward the light.

The title, *flowering*, speaks to this universal process. It is not merely the act of blooming that defines us, but the entire journey—rooted in darkness, breaking through soil, reaching for light, and eventually releasing what no longer serves us. This is a collection about embracing the entirety of that process, in all its imperfect beauty. Each poem is a step in that journey, a moment that captures introduction

an emotional truth, whether it be pain, joy, anger, or acceptance.

This collection is built around the belief that growth is not linear. Just as in nature, where each plant, tree, or flower has its own unique cycle, so too do we experience life's challenges and triumphs on our own terms, in our own time. The titles of the poems—borrowed from languages across the world—reflect this diversity, capturing nuanced emotions that defy simple translation. Whether it is the bittersweet scent of *sillage*, or the warmth of *apricity* on a winter's day, these words invite the reader to pause and consider the many ways we experience life's moments of beauty and hardship.

As you enter the world of *flowering*, I encourage you to see these poems as moments that stand apart but also connect to one another. Some may resonate deeply, while others may reflect a more distant truth. Each is a small reflection of the broader journey we are all on—a journey of becoming, of letting go, and of blooming into ourselves.

prologue

flowering:

[adjective]

1. producing or bearing flowers.
2. covered with or full of flowers.

[noun]

1. the act or state of producing flowers.
2. an unfolding development.
3. a flourishing state of period of new development and growth.

sunrise

[noun] the rising of the sun above the horizon that floods the sky with light.

And so it begins.
Like the sun that creeps from behind the sea
so far from me.
Like the light that inches forward
every hour and minute and second.
Like the tangible sense of joy and renewal and hope
from the shining star across.

Life.
Birth.
Sunrise.

selcouth

[adjective] unfamiliar, rare, strange, and yet wondrous

They flash red and blue and green,
and every shade besides.
They weave and dance and run,
blinding in the unending, enveloping black sky.
They play and fight and clash,
filling every dark crevice and corner
with flares of blazing lights.

They cry of oddity,
of lightning that is not lightning.
They sing of the unknown,
of the heights of the skies and the size of the cosmos.
They hum for wonder,
of the wheel of colours splintering
into uncountable fragments in the heavens.

They are strange and peculiar and haunting.
They are mesmerising and curious and foreign.

They are new and unpredictable and beautiful.

kalopsia

[noun] the delusion of things being more beautiful than they really are

She stands in her solitude:
a siren of the sea,
a singer to damned souls.
Soothing and mesmerizing,
captivating and enrapturing,
as her voice rings and

echoes

                        echoes

                                              echoes

Scales glitter and reflect secrets of the sea
glimmering, shimmering upon tall cave walls.
Hair of the sun,
Skin of snow,
An anomaly of beauty, a paradoxical kalon.
A picture of seduction.
One cannot help but stare, gawk, long
for the object of one's
Desires.
She calls and enthralls.

flowering

Hypnotized by her voice, tinkling music box of allure,
walk, run, crawl
towards the voice of lust:
irresistible and enchanting,
dreams of all that is craved for,
visions of all that could be.
Luring with sweet nothings,
whisperings of songs in the winds:
Entice me, take me,
make me everything you want.

> my mother
> no, my lost sister
> no, my dead lover
> no, my slipping betrothed
> mine, mine, mine
> not yours, mine
> cries of possession, thuds of feet on planks
> resounding, maddening
> minds enveloped by greedy sand
> that occupies every corner
> mine, mine, mine
> I said it already, did you not hear?
> Let me make it clear:
> M I N E.

Men sail, women sail.
Men yearn, women yearn.

kalopsia

Men drown, women drown
in their watery graves.
Their siren invites.
Magnetized hearts of iron,
footsteps controlled by a puppeteer
of veils and deception and death.
She entraps their hearts, she captures their eyes.
She owns their being.
She squeezes their life out of their vulnerable shells.
She delivers her judgement on ravenous shipmates
driven apart by desire.

One stands apart.
Rubber stoppers silence trances.
He will not cave, he will not surrender:
"I will not crumble to her songs.
She may try to claim me,
with her lullabies of beauty and elegance,
but I see through with my pure eyes.
I see through your lies to your promises of death.
I see your goals just as you see theirs.
I will show you.

Do you see her?
She promises you love. She promises you life.
She promises all you crave for.
Do you not see
the sharp edges of blood-dripping, slow murder songs?
Look at the venal plea

flowering

                      hidden by her lilting, bewitching voice,
                      the treacherous whirpools and currents
                      she hides with traitorous white sands,
                      her gauzy veils of deceit.
Can you not see claws beneath porcelain-plain gloves?
Can you not see glistening fangs beneath cherry full lips?
Can you not see snakes as they wrap around her head?
                      Can you not see? Or do you wish to not?

                      Stay away, plug your ears.
                      Do not be swayed by smothering voices.
                      Do not be campaigned by pretense.
                      Do not lose your melodies of truth:
                      Hum through the dissuading pitches of death,
                      sing your songs of loyalty, dedication, integrity.
                      Do not lose your way, do not give her way.
                      Do not accept, do not falter.
                      be

                      o n e."

        Warnings are often shown indifference.
        Roses are the blood-lusting truths:
        thorns are all that prompt change.
     Pandora's opened box with trapped Hope,
          who must be allowed to escape,
         but is chained down by negligence.
        Just as the sea changes her mind,

kalopsia

just as the siren who may captivate or murder,
sailors who set sail but run adrift, cannot steer their ships
to safety:
For why should they listen to the soft lowly pleas of a deck-
hand?

She stands in all her glory:
they see their saviour.
They sail, they dive, they swim.
They are entangled in venomous snakes of ivy that drag

down

down

down

until they reach the depths of darkness,
where all that is seen are monsters and creatures that
nightmares are made of.
She whispers to them love-promises of oblivion,
as she slits, with her now revealed claws,
and tears through the tears
of the one who knew, but was ignored.

parasite

[noun] one that leeches off and drains its host

The tendril slithered towards the tiny sapling:
a new life
reaching for the sun,
unfurling to the sky.

It coils around the child:
unsuspecting
and innocent,
welcoming a friend.

The young sprout embraces its approach:
a fellow traveller
questing for a sunkissed promise,
a serpentine comrade in arms.

The vine's persistent threads tighten:
an ever-hastening
intertwining of fate,
foreshadowing a rise and fall.

flowering

Rope clenches around the confused throat:
the fledgling unanticipatedly
unable to breathe
in the constricting arms of a once-friend.

Snakes inhaled the warmth of new soulfire:
intoxicating youth
scrumptious to the taste,
a renewed source of entrancing breath.

The fingers gripped even harder:
a secured prize
forever overpowered,
and swelled twofold.

The yarn wove its tapestry thick:
it concealed all evidence
of an ill-earned triumph,
unleashing the limp, drained sprout.

It flopped, tumbling into its losing void:
the victor arose atop
and craned its neck
searching for its next victim.

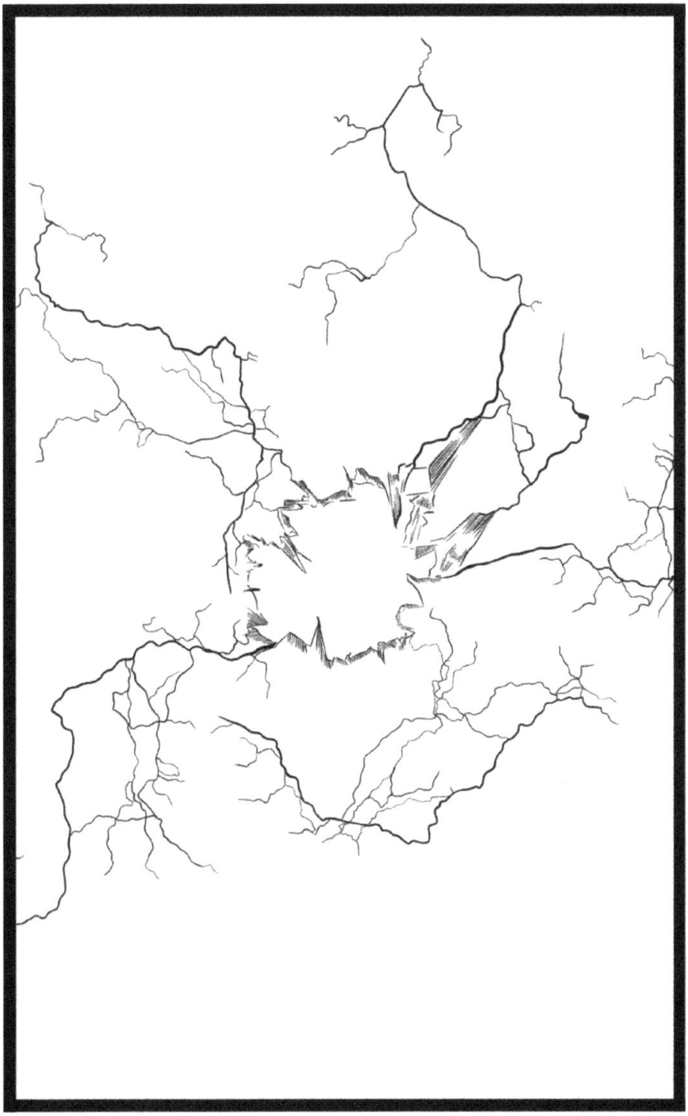

agowilt

[noun] an uncontrollable, sudden, sickening fear

Fear.
My heart beats faster;
it's going to jump out of my chest.
Thunder rumbles in a warning roar,
The earth shakes in dread and apprehension,
The air is thick and tense, suffocating.
I can't think. I can't breathe.
Where am I?
What is this?
Help me, I'm scared.
I can't see. It's all blurring together, like smothering smog.
Why is the ground swaying beneath my feet?
I'm so dizzy.
Why are there black spots?
Someone, please.
My knees hit the dirt.
There's blinding pain.
Make it stop.
I can't hear anything.
I can only feel a pounding in my chest,
so loud that I might combust.
It's so heavy, take it away!

flowering

Why is the thunder so loud?
Please!
I can't be here, I can't do this!
Please.
Please!
Stop it.
Help me!
Please.
Why is my face wet?
Please.
Someone, please!

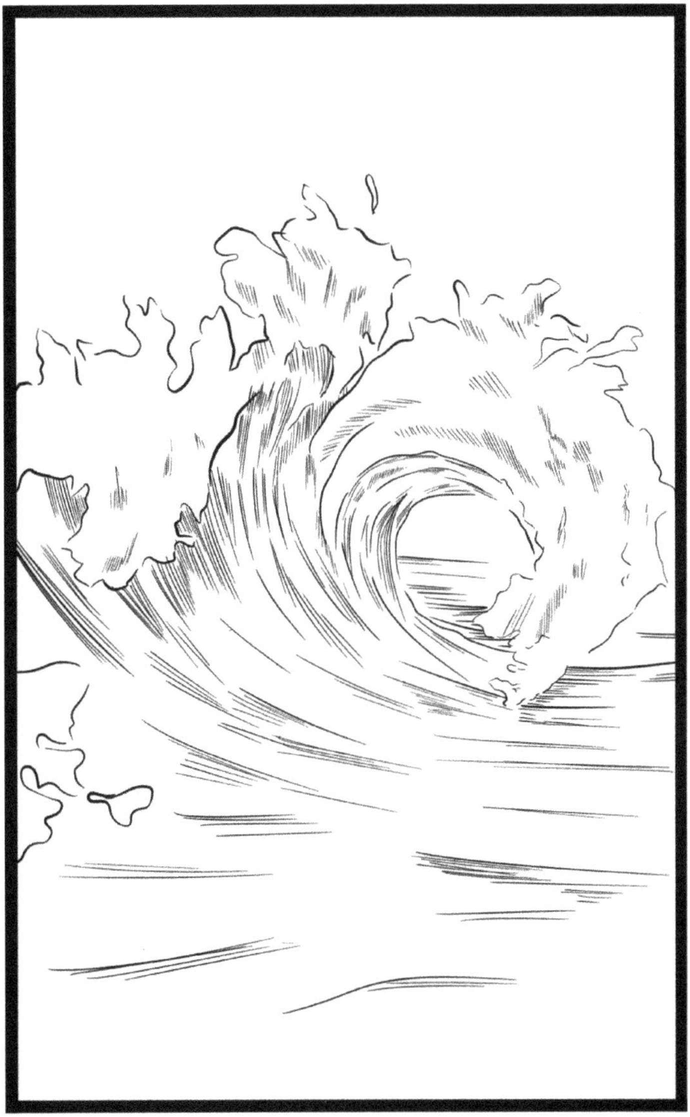

douleur

[noun] misery, anguish, and excruciating pain

The unforeseeable approach of a wall of charging water,
a ruthless tidal tempest, an uncontrollable, swarming marauder.
Swifter than rain but incomparably stronger,
nothing protected from callous slaughter.

The ocean's inexorable wrath ravenously consumed
everything in sight till all that was, was entombed.
Ubiquitous agony and enveloping torment ensued,
choking and bruised, battering and abused.

Unrelenting.
Nightmarish.
Brutal.
Eviscerating.
Acerbic.
Ripping.
Assailing.
Breaking.
Lacerating.
Enslaving.

HURT.

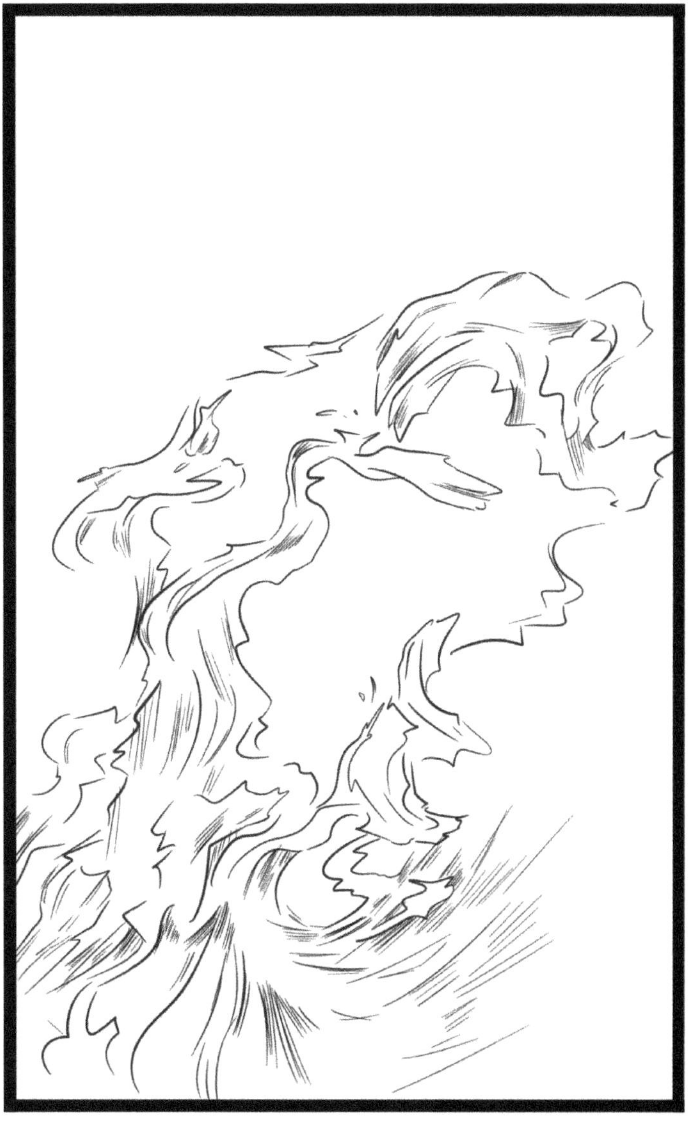

rancour

[noun] bitter resentment, malice, and deep-seated, all-consuming hatred

Take back what is owed.
Burn and burn.

Devour and eradicate.
Burn and burn.

Hate the hands that did it.
Burn and burn.

Annihilate its very existence.
Burn and burn.

Growl and snarl and ravage and shred.
Burn and burn.

Hiss in venomous, smoky intent.
Burn and burn.

flowering

Tear it all down.
Burn and burn.

Roar until nothing stands.
Burn and burn.

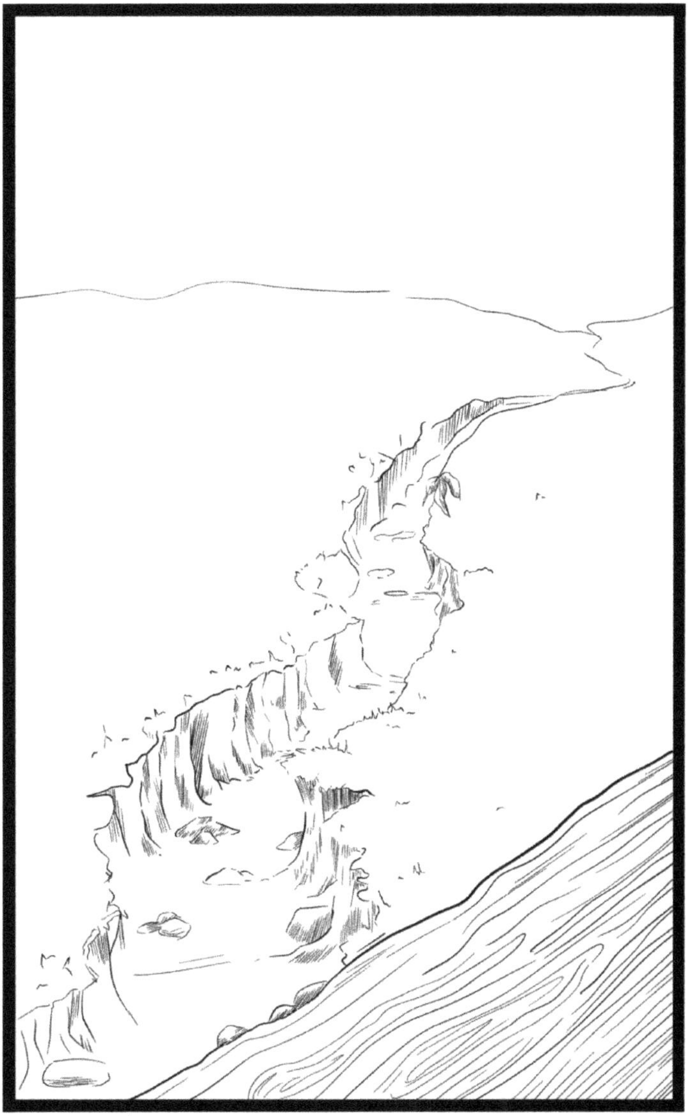

lacuna

[noun] a blank space, a missing part

When all is gone and none remains,
When rain is lost and life is drained,
When the nightingale ceases to sing her refrains,
I whisper to myself in the silence.

When my rivers are sand and no longer so sweet,
When the clouds and the wind have accepted defeat,
When all that was is made obsolete,
I whisper to myself in the silence.

When the will is dead as the way has been,
When the emptiness is inescapable and the air is thin,
When all is gone and all is barren,
I stare into the distance in the silence.

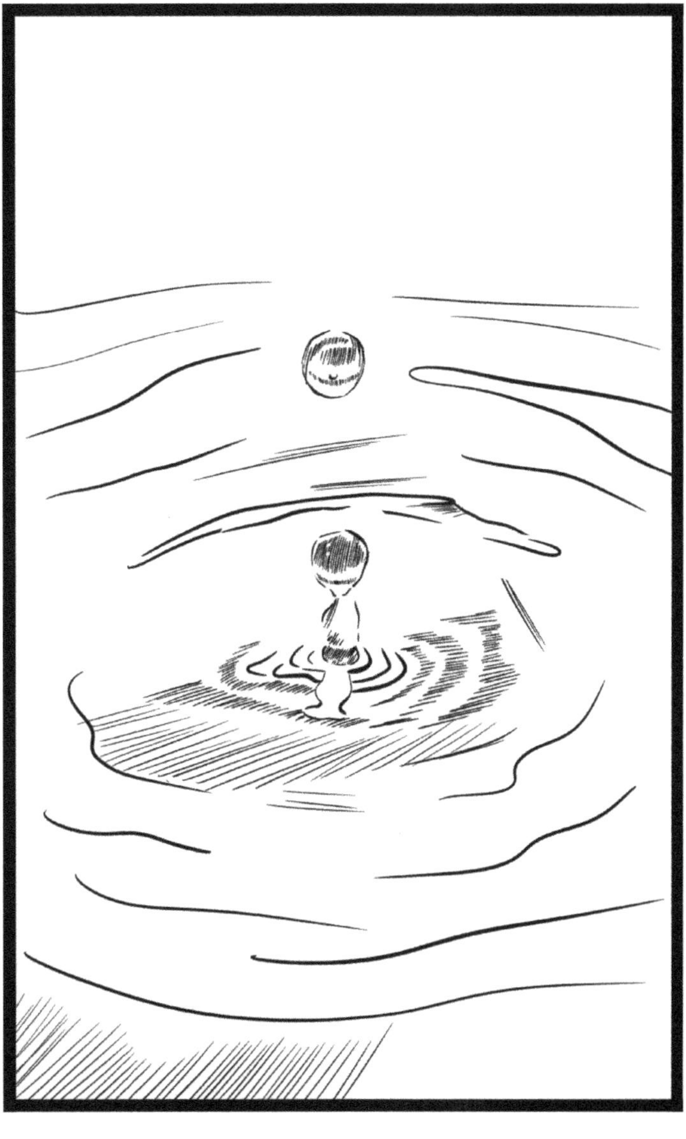

petrichor

[noun] the smell of the earth after rain

The sky had wept softly,
a quiet drizzle on parched ground,
each drop readily, hungrily
absorbed
into the thirsty soil
with no resistance.

Alone, the earth breathed in,
holding the memory
of the rain
and its embrace
as a solitary scent
lingering
long after the clouds had passed.

The world was still,
hushed,
and even the wind
hesitated
to flutter the leaves
as if
mourning
the loss of touch.

flowering

The scent of
petrichor
now rises,
a bittersweet perfume
of what once had been
and does not remain,
for even the earth knows
the ache
of solitude.

Loneliness is
what I call
the quiet
after the rain,
when the earth
sighs
beneath a sky once filled
with the promise of connection,
now left
to dry
and die
in the silence.

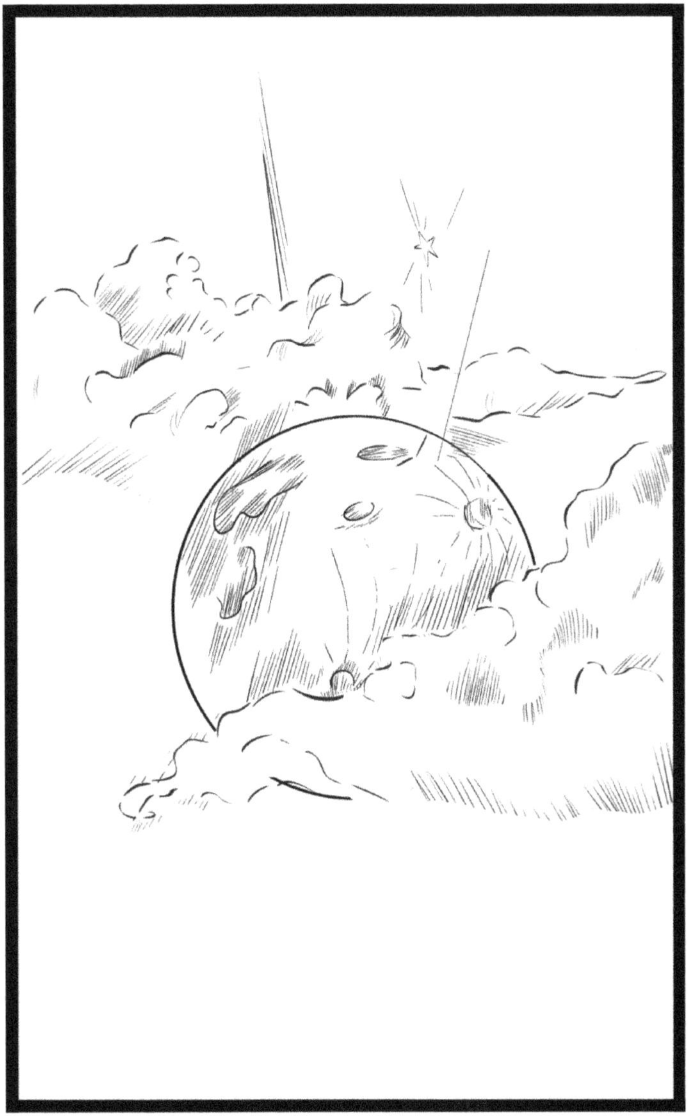

desvelado

[adjective] sleepless

The cold distant moon hung
in a cloudless, empty sky.

The relentless waves
crashed quietly
on a deserted
moonlit shore.

The shadows of sparse foliage
cast by moonlight
shifted and flickered
on a craggy, rocky surface.

The thin, cold mist
rose slowly
in tendrils
above the dark waters
in the dead
of night.

The day creatures slumbered
in the silence,
peacefully,

flowering

while the nocturnal awoke
subtly, imperceptibly,
rustling the underbrush.

The sky clouded softly
with a veil of healing gauze
as a single, faint star
struggled to shine,
lonely, far away
on the horizon,
glimmering once it could be seen.

And the cold distant moon hung
in a starry, wispy sky,
as the quiet of the night
spoke softly of hope.

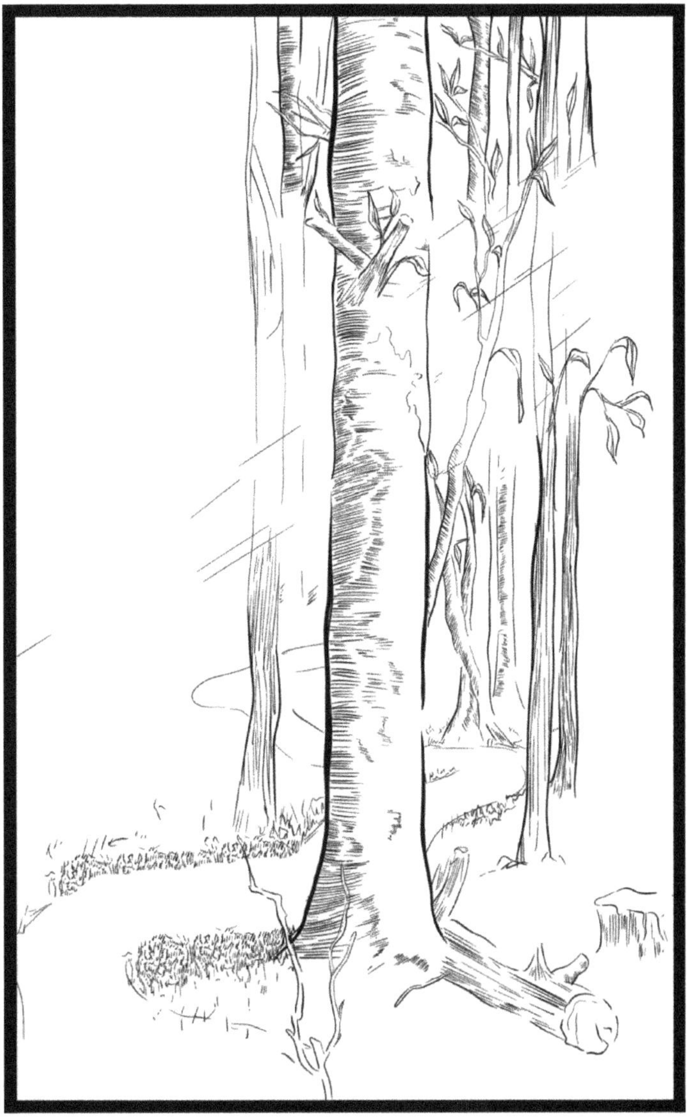

komorebi

[noun] the play of sunlight through the leaves

A gentle breeze
stirred the leaves,
whispering prophecies
of soon to come
light.

The leaves rustled softly,
their edges aglow
as the forest rumbled
awakened by touches
of a coming day.

Soft beams of light
filtered through the green,
dancing tenderly
on the forest floor.

Morning dew clung
gingerly
to the edges of green folioles,
each droplet a prism
turning sunlight
into rainbows.

flowering

Golden patches of warmth
kiss
the moss-covered ground,
where shadows
once held sway.

A narrow path winds through the woods
as a golden ribbon of light
unfurling into the heart
of this awakened, illuminated world.

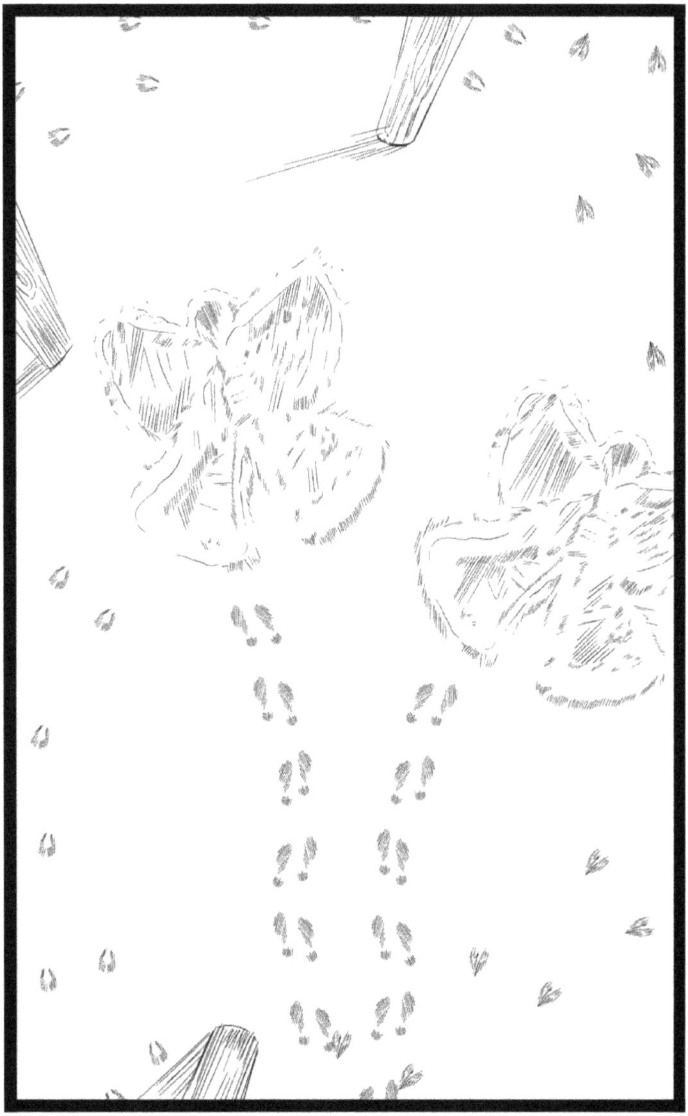

apricity

[noun] the warmth of the sun in winter

In the heart
of winter
when the earth lay
still
beneath a blanket of frost,
you came,
the sun,
peeking through heavy clouds,
casting your golden light
on a world
otherwise steeped in
grey.

The air,
once brittle with cold,
softened
at your
delicate,
caressing,
comforting
touch:
a warmth so gentle

flowering

it was almost a whisper,
a breath of life
in the silence of snow.

You were
morning light,
slipping through frost-laden branches,
turning icicles to diamonds,
painting the world
with a brilliance
it had forgotten.

Under your gracing gaze,
the snow
began to shimmer,
each flake catching
the light
and reflecting
a thousand tiny suns.

The frozen river
stirred
beneath its glassy surface,
its slow
hidden current,
now alive
with
possibility.

apricity

In the forest,
where shadows
slowly lost their reign,
you brought
a delicate
glow,
a softness,
a loveliness,
that coaxed the first buds
from their winter sleep,
tender green
with a promise
held within
the warming cold.

I walked with you
through a world
newly awakened,
where every breath
was a mingling
of crisp air
and warmth,
delightful warmth,
where the sun dipped low,
but never lost its fire
where the earth,
though wrapped
in an icy winter's cloak,

flowering

began to dream
of spring.

The snow,
once stark and silent,
became a canvas
for the patterns
of the footsteps
of the deer
and the little rabbits
and the waking,
each step a gentle imprint
on soft
yielding surface,
each moment
each press
each step
a dance
fleetingly flying between
chill and an
overwhelmingly
mesmerizingly
entrancingly
captivatingly
lulling
warmth.

The wind,
though sharp,

carried the
intermingling scents
of pine and cedar and oak,
but
beneath it,
a hint
of something
sweeter,
like the memory of summer
clinging
to the edges
of winter's rasping breath.

The day waned,
and the sky blushed
with the colours
of dusk
tingeing the snow
a myriad of warm shades
from the palest apricot
to the brightest coral,
a gradient reflection
of the setting sun.
The warmth
of your presence
lingered
like these last rays of sunlight
before nightfall,
a quiet comfort

flowering

against
the encroaching dark.

Yet
even as night fell,
the cold retreating
under a blanket of constellations and stars,
that warmth of yours
did not fade,
but nestled deeper,
beneath the surface of things,
kindling a secret fire
in the heart of winter,
waking and loving and rearing.

The moon rose,
a silver sentinel
against the velvet sky,
its light
a soft caress
on the snow-laden ground,
and still
there you were,
your warmth spreading
entangling
with the night air,
no longer so frigid,
turning the frost
into a soft

apricity

shimmering glow,
a quiet luminescence
that danced despite
the shadows.

The trees,
their branches bare,
etched delicate patterns
against the night,
and the world,
bathed in your
gentle
adoring
light,
breathed
in unison
with the steady pulse
of waking hearts
in the earth beneath.

We wandered,
hand in hand,
yours in mine,
mine in yours,
through this twilight world,
your presence
constant,
like the steady glow of embers
refusing to die,

flowering

even as night deepened
and the cold wolf
sharpened
its unsheathed claws.

The stars watched
over us,
their light
a chorus
of distant fires,
and
in their glow,
I found a reflection
of the warmth you brought
to my winter days,
a warmth that seeped
into every corner
of my very being
and each bone
tendon
and ligament
of this wintery landscape,
as you transformed it
from cold,
unfeeling, freezing, crying cold,
to living
breathing
earth.

As the hours stretched
into the small moments
of night,
I could feel
the first stirrings
of dawn,
a promise carried
on the back
of the unflinching wind,
whispering of another day
when your warmth
your sun
your light
your love
would rise again
and with it,
you.

And even though the endless night
was long,
it was never lonely,
not even for a moment,
for your presence
was a constant flame
a constant thawing
a steadiness
that held me close
even as my world
slept beneath

flowering

its winter shroud.
And so we remained,
entwined,
in the quiet
fulfilling embrace
of first love's gentle fire,
a warmth that did not fade,
would never fade,
refused to fade,
despite the darkness,
the cold,
the biting emptiness,
but instead
grew stronger
with every passing moment.
A light that turned even
the coldest night
to a sanctuary
of warmth,
a place where the world
paused
and we,
together,
basked in our love.

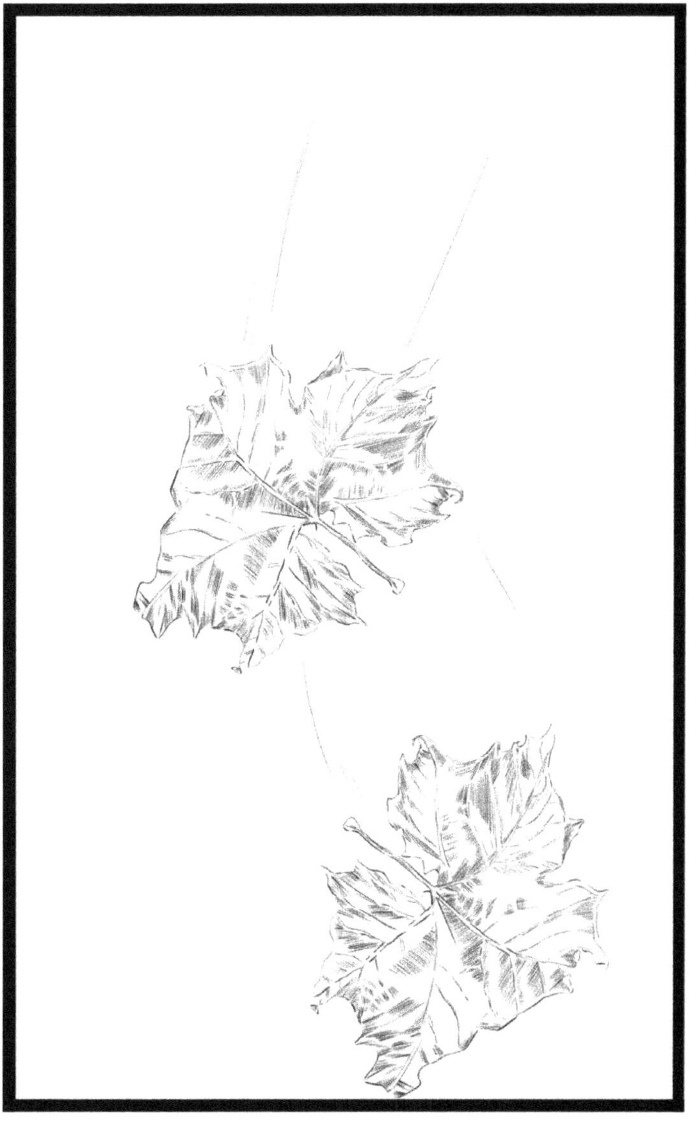

sillage

[noun] the scent that lingers in the air, the impression left in space after something or someone has been and gone

The leaves descend gently in autumn's whispered hush,
Golden remnants of a summer's long-lost fire, now dim and gray,
A fleeting, fragrant ghost that lingers in the brush.

Bare branches stretch like ancient arms in solemn flush,
Their verdant robes surrendered to the sway of time's decay,
The leaves descend gently in autumn's whispered hush.

A mournful wind, a lover's breath, gives the forest one last blush,
Carrying whispers of a passion once ablaze, now turned to clay,
A fleeting, fragrant ghost that lingers in the brush.

Each step through the paths of crimson fall feels like a quiet rush,
As brittle leaves crumble and scrunch underfoot, like memories frayed and gray,
The leaves descend gently in autumn's whispered hush.

flowering

The amber fields now lie in tender, rusted lush,
As autumn's hand paints every bough in hues that fade away,
A fleeting, fragrant ghost that lingers in the brush.

The orchard trees, once rich with life, now bend and groan and shush,
Their boughs weighed down by fruitless thoughts, and colours gone to stay-
The leaves descend gently in autumn's whispered hush,
A fleeting, fragrant ghost that lingers in the brush.

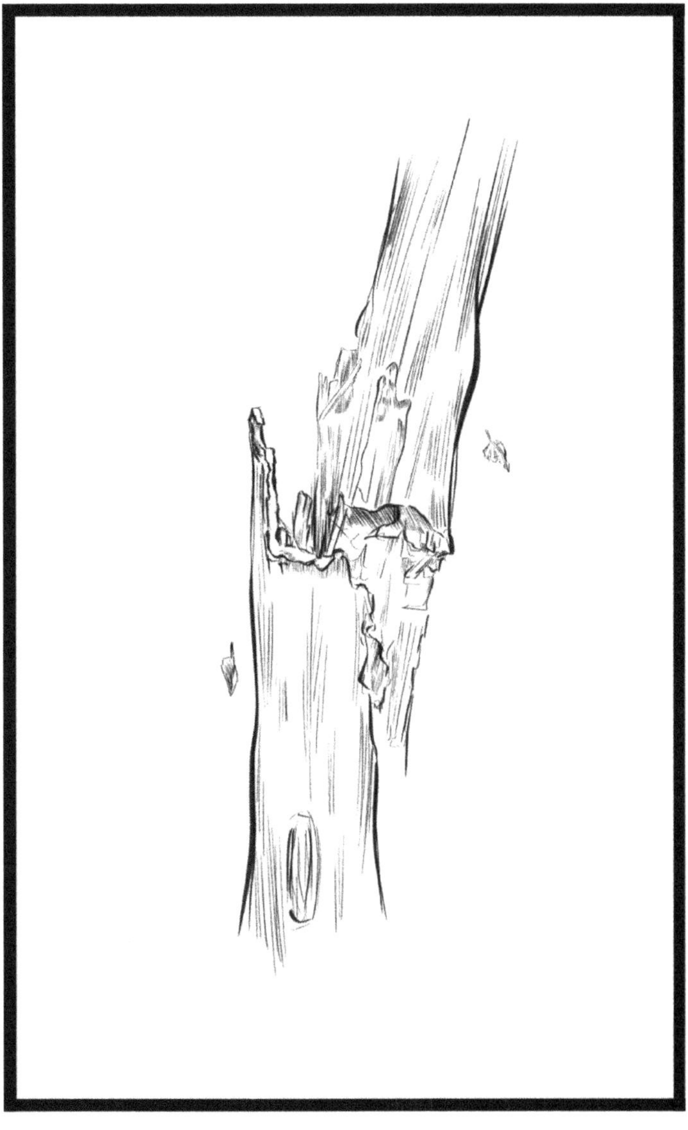

cicatrize

[verb] to find healing by the process of forming scars

Beneath the storm's inexorable gaze,
The ancient oak, once proud in verdant bloom,
Was cleaved asunder, like a lover's heart.
Its bark, erstwhile so smooth, was marred by fate,
A scar that traced the pain endured.

Yet from that wound, where dolour's shadow fell,
A nascent grace emerged, a balm divine.
The sap, like liquid gold, began to flow,
With whispered vows of healing in its path.
Nature, in her taciturn, steadfast way,
Did weave her magic through the sundered wood,
And what was riven grew a sacred seam,
A mark where strength and beauty intertwined.

The branches bowed, like mourners in the wind,
Yet did not splinter under tempest's might.
They bore the weight of woe, but did not break,
And from the scar, new life began to bloom.
Soft leaves of green unfurled, kissed by the dawn,
And in their dance, the light of hope was born.
The oak, now graced with scars of silent pride,

flowering

Stood tall, a testament to what survived.
For in each groove, a tale of love and loss,
Of battles won despite the weight of time,
A chronicle of wounds that healed through grace,
Of pain transformed into a strength sublime.

No cure was sought from foreign, fleeting hands,
No remedy but time's enduring flow.
The tree, with wisdom from life's trials earned,
Found in itself the means to mend and grow.
The scar, a silvered line upon the bark,
Spoke not of what was lost, but what was gained—
A fortitude that in the dark did spark,
A love that, though once bruised, remained unstained.

And so the oak, its grandeur undiminished,
By storm and time and trials unforeseen,
Now stands in quietude, its scars adorned,
With symbols of the strength that had been earned.
The wound, once raw, now gleams with softened light,
A symbol not of loss, but of rebirth,
A proof that in the gloaming of the night,
The soul can find its way back to the earth.
For scars, though born of sorrow's deepest kiss,
Are but the seals of life's enduring bliss.

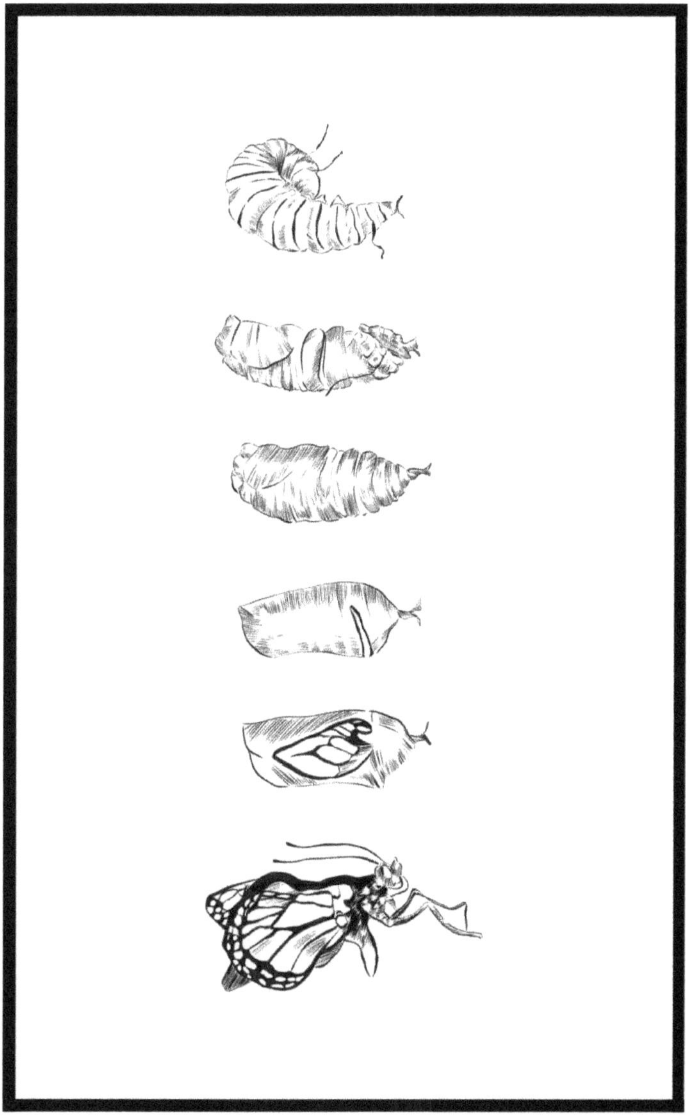

metanoia

[noun] the journey of changing one's mind, heart, self, or way of life

She is.
She begins.
She breathes.

She quivered in the black endless nothing.
She pushed against the oozy slime and emerged.

She crawled slowly on the branch, determined to reach the leaf.
It hung limply in the distance, calling to her with every step.

It might have taken minutes, hours, days or years.
Time flew as she inched towards its sacred glow.

It was soft.
It was tender.
It was full of life.

She dove into its vastness, all-consuming.
Except, she was the one that consumed it.

flowering

It gave her strength and vitality, and she felt herself change in that moment.
She paused where the leaf once stood, suspended in the crisp air.

It began gently, and then continued hastily, all at once until she was covered and enveloped in a cocoon of her own making.

It was dark.
It was silent.
It was peaceful comfort.

She nestled in the warmth, held close by threads of her own design,
Safe in the knowledge of who she had been.
Yet something called from beyond the silken walls,
A whisper of the world waiting in the light.
She felt a shift in her back, a shift in her limbs,
a difference of weight, yet weightless and still.

Something was new.

It was strange and unusual, but familiar,
an old friend never made.

But it was not time.
She waited, patient as life in the permafrost.

And then it began to bloom.

Slowly, gently, a flower of life and rebirth.
Colourfully, vividly, she awakes.

Her iridescent wings of glory sprang free,
her antennae unfurled with a twirl.
The colours of the waves and the tides of the sea,
a mirror of the currents that swirl.

She was strong, and she was bold.
She was grandeur to behold.
No longer was she weak or dull
or held back in predefined limits.
She was luminous and glistening and turquoise,
unrestrained in her confident joy.

She pushed back with her wings
and took to the sky.
Hidden and forgotten, her struggle,
as she flew on high.

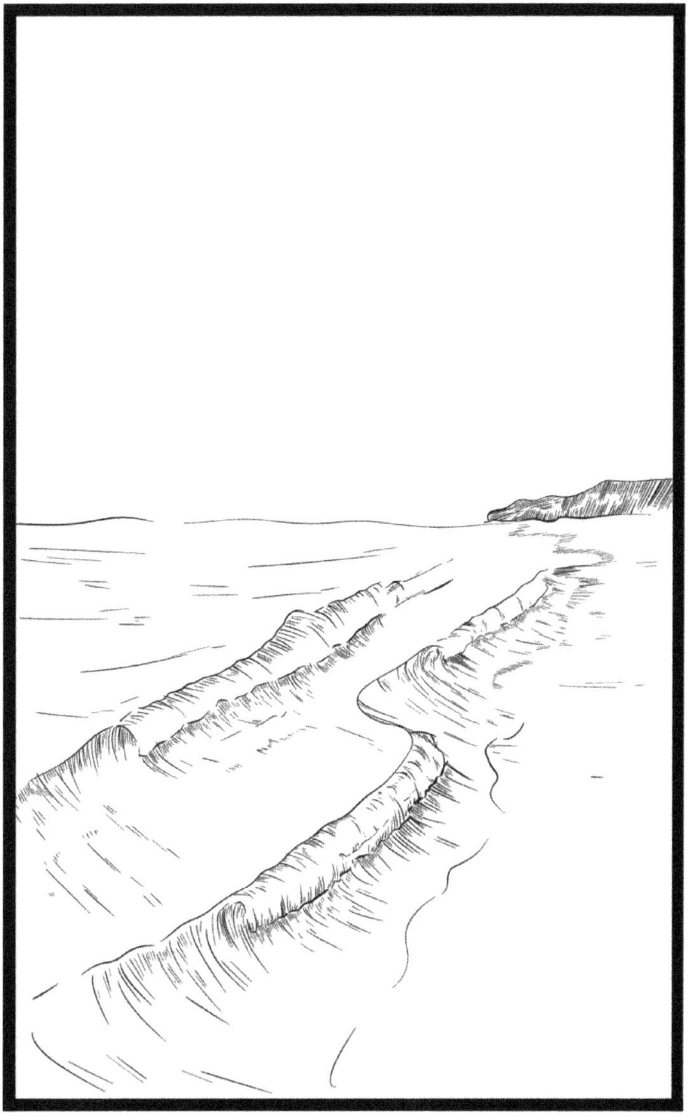

koi no yokan

[noun] the feeling upon first meeting someone that you will inevitably fall in love

The ocean stirs beneath the crescent moon,
Its waves, a whisper soft upon the night,
Drawn ever closer by the tides' own tune.

Each crest, a breath, as day surrenders light,
And sends its tender touch toward the shore,
Where sands await the sea's encroaching flight.

With every surge, the heart of the shore begins to soar,
For in this dance of water, earth, and sky,
A love foreseen arrives with gentle lore.

No fear, no haste, as waves are drawn nearby,
For shore and sea in timeless rhythm meet,
To blend their worlds beneath the open sky.

The shore receives the sea's embrace with peace,
A union whispered by the stars above,
As I await the tide that brings release.

The tides will rise- I welcome you, my love.

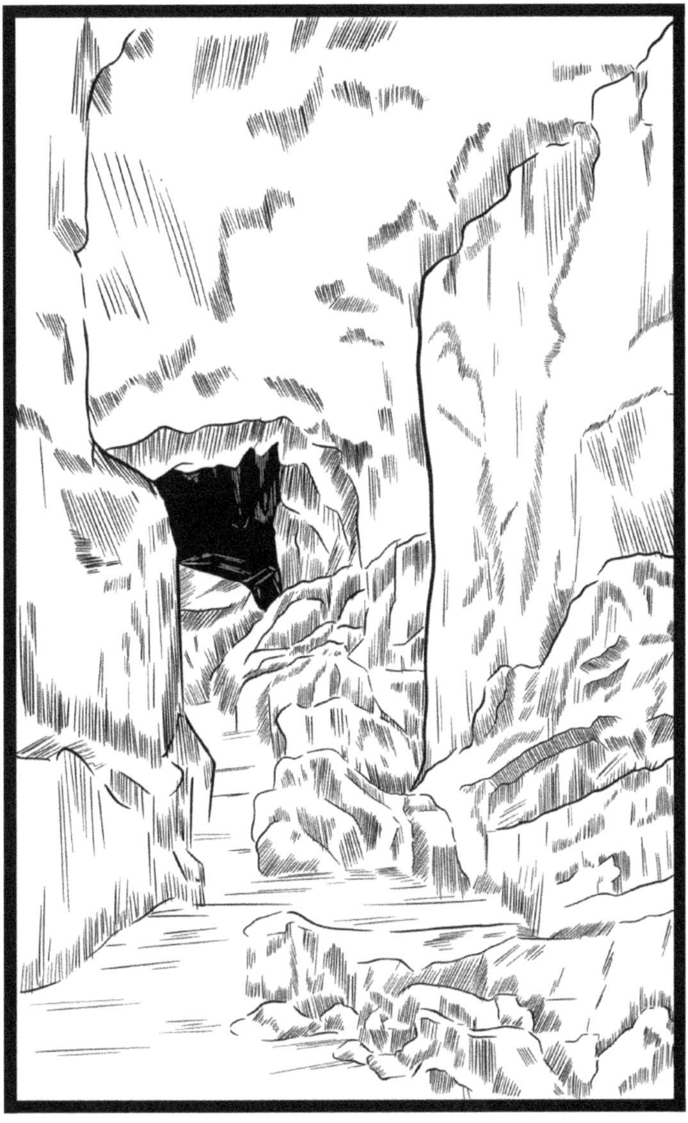

querencia

[noun] a place, and home, from which one's strength is drawn to be their authentic self

In twilight's glow, the cove enfolds with grace,
A hidden world where whispers of the sea
Embrace the shore, like lovers, face to face,
Their union soft, a tender reverie.
The walls, aglow with light's celestial trace,
Reflect the dance of waves in harmony,
Here, in this place where earth and ocean meet,
I find a peace that time could not defeat.

The tide rolls in, a kiss upon the land,
As moonlight drapes its silver on the waves,
Each ripple sings of nature's gentle hand,
A song that echoes deep within these caves.
The ocean's voice, both quiet and so grand,
Resounds in every chamber, every nave,
Within this cove, the world is stilled, serene,
Where hearts entwine, and all the stars convene.

Beneath the vaulted sky, where dreams take flight,
The water's edge, a cradle for the night,
Each moment here, a shimmer of delight,
A testament to what feels pure and right.

flowering

The walls around me glow with softest light,
Where every wave reflects a secret vow,
In this embrace, there is no end in sight,
For here, I'm held by all I've dreamed of now.

The sea, it breathes with tender, endless sigh,
A rhythm found in every pulse, each beat,
No longer do I search, no longer try,
For in this cove, my soul is made complete.
The waters lap, a gentle lullaby,
A melody where sky and ocean meet,
And in this place, my spirit starts to soar,
To find the depth that I've been longing for.

No walls could hold the passion in these waves,
No boundaries could contain the ocean's heart,
For in this cove, the sea with each pulse craves,
To merge with earth, no longer torn apart.
The rocks and tides, in endless dance, behave
As those who meet, who never wish to part,
And in this meeting of the sea and stone,
I find a bond much deeper than my own.

Here, time dissolves, the past and future fade,
The present is a blissful, endless now,
Where what is felt in every light and shade,
Is soft as night, yet strong as any vow.
The ocean's depth, in moonlit glow displayed,
Reveals the truth that time would not allow,

Yet here it blooms, in every wave and crest,
A sense of something real, at last expressed.

The cove, it holds the secrets of the sea,
The waves, they know the truth that hearts impart,
For in this place, the world feels wild and free,
Where earth and ocean join in one deep heart.
Each glimmer on the water speaks to me,
Of something deep, enduring, set apart,
And as I stand within this hallowed space,
I know I've found my spirit's resting place.

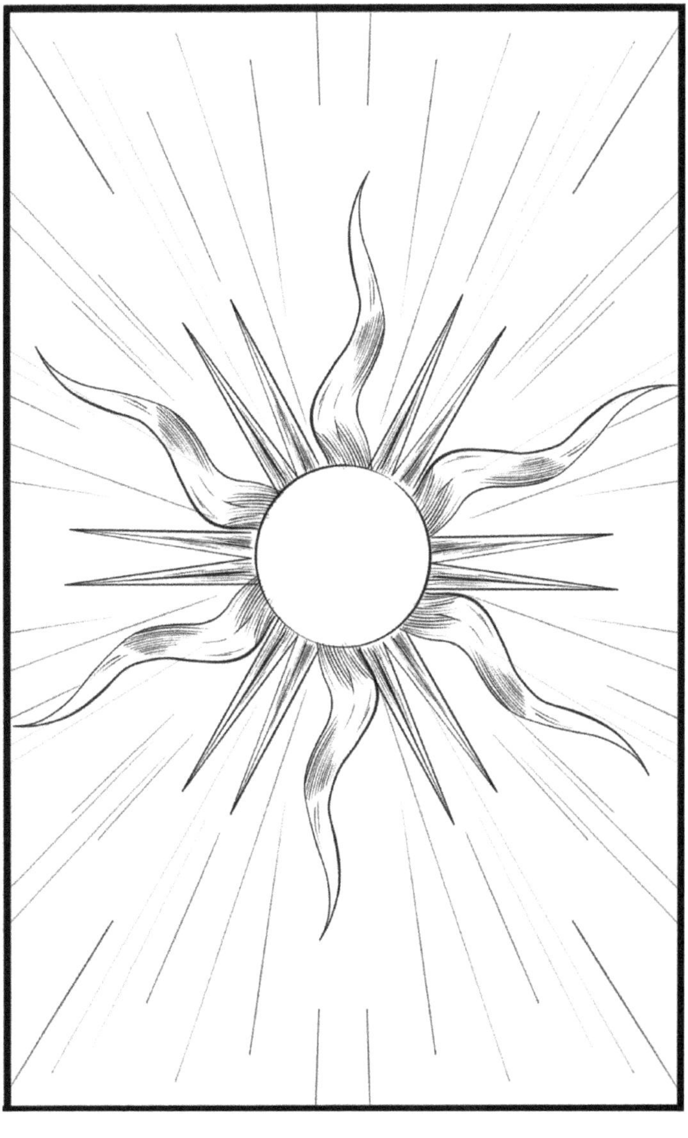

raison d'être

[noun] one's reason for existing and living

The sun ascends, a sovereign in the sky,
Its golden fire ignites the world below,
With every ray, it breathes a fervent sigh,
A life-giving pulse, a steady, endless flow.
Across the heavens, in its grand array,
It sweeps the stars aside, commands the day,
A beacon bright, the heart of all that lives,
Its light the gift that all creation gives.

From dawn's first blush, the sky's warm caress,
The sun begins its journey, vast and true,
A chariot of flame, with no regress,
Its path a line that cuts the endless blue.
It draws the world in orbit 'round its fire,
Each life a thread within its glowing spire,
For in its blaze, all things find form and place,
A dance of time, a cosmic, endless grace.

The mountains rise to greet its gentle light,
Their peaks ablaze with gold at morning's touch,
The valleys wake beneath its warming sight,
As shadows flee before its grasping clutch.

flowering

The oceans stir, their surfaces aglow,
Reflecting back the sun's majestic show,
In every wave, a piece of light remains,
A whispered echo of its vast domains.

The forests sway beneath the sun's command,
Their leaves turned upward, seeking every beam,
The fields of grain, they ripen on the land,
Each stalk a product of the sun's bright gleam.
In deserts wide, where only sand prevails,
The sun's embrace is harsh, yet never fails,
It sculpts the dunes, it shapes the barren plain,
And even here, its power does sustain.

The creatures of the earth all know its call,
From smallest insect to the greatest beast,
They rise and rest within its daily thrall,
Their lives a feast of light that never ceased.
The birds, they soar on wings of purest gold,
Their songs a tribute to the sun's great hold,
And in the depths, where shadows seek their prey,
The sun's faint touch still guides the hunter's way.

The flowers bloom beneath its tender gaze,
Each petal kissed by light, its colors born,
The meadows stretch in vast, unbroken praise,
Their verdant carpets spread at every dawn.
The rivers run, their currents swift and sure,
Carved by the sun's relentless, bright allure,

And in each drop, the sunlight finds a home,
A spark of life within the water's foam.

As day progresses, sun climbs ever high,
Its zenith reached in blinding, brilliant flare,
The world beneath, it basks in midday's eye,
A kingdom ruled by light beyond compare.
No corner left untouched by its embrace,
No shadow can withstand its fervent chase,
And in this moment, all the earth does see,
The sun's true power, boundless, pure, and free.

Yet even as the sun begins to wane,
Its light a softer glow in evening's tide,
It leaves behind a world both rich and plain,
A land where night and day in peace reside.
The sunset's hues, they paint the sky with fire,
A blaze of color that the heart inspires,
And as it sinks, the sun does gently leave,
A promise of return that we believe.

The moon ascends, its silver light so pale,
A mirror to the sun's more potent flame,
Yet even in the night, the sun prevails,
Its echoes in the stars that share its name.
For every star is but a distant sun,
A beacon shining through the void undone,
And in their light, the sun's great truth is found,
A reason for existence, pure and sound.

flowering

The earth itself, it turns within its grasp,
A planet held in place by sun's command,
Its orbit drawn by sun's unyielding clasp,
A path defined by forces grand and planned.
The seasons change, the years, they come and go,
Each cycle marked by sun's unending glow,
For in its fire, all life finds meaning true,
A constant light that guides the old and new.

And as the sun begins its rise again,
To chase away the shadows of the night,
The world awakens with a joyous grin,
To greet the dawn, the source of all its might.
The mountains, seas, and forests know its name,
The creatures sing, their lives an endless flame,
And in the heart of every living thing,
The sun's bright fire is felt, a constant ring.

For in the sun, the world finds all it needs,
A reason to exist, a cause to strive,
Its light the source from which all life proceeds,
The spark that keeps the universe alive.
No greater force, no truer guide exists,
No deeper truth than what the sun insists,
That life is found within its warm embrace,
A beacon bright in every time and place.

The sun, it rises, never will it fall,
Its light a constant in the skies above,

raison d'être

And in its glow, the world will heed its call,
For in its fire, we find our endless love.
The sun ascends, a truth that none can mar,
A burning heart, our ever-guiding star,
For in its light, we find our reason why,
Our raison d'être, beneath the endless sky.

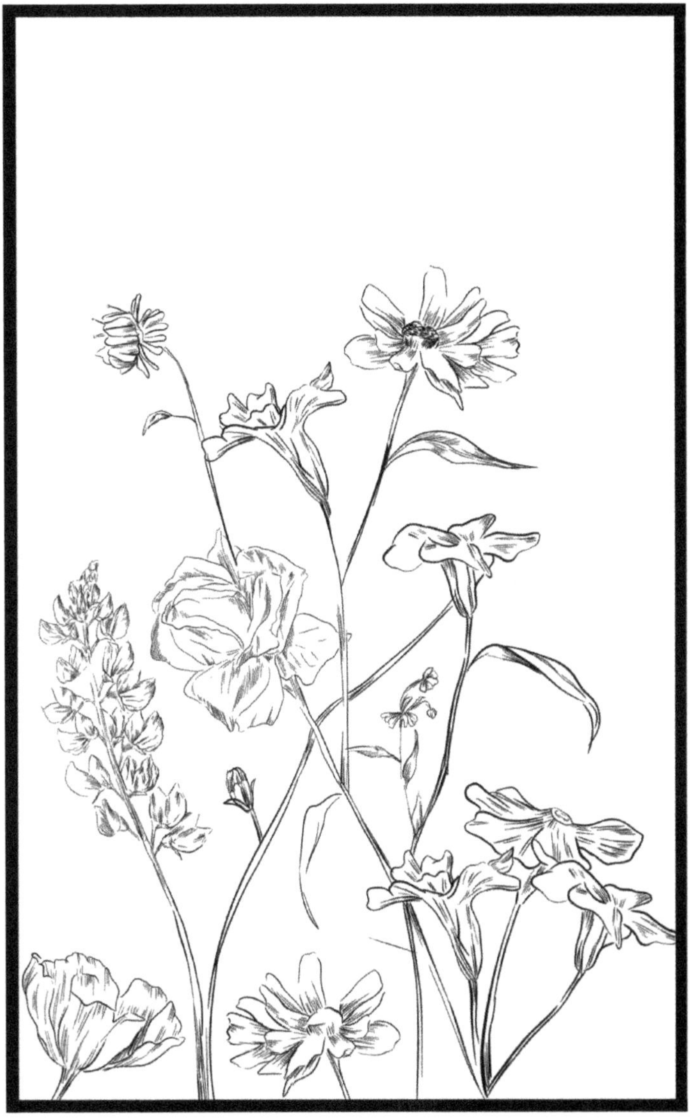

oubaitori

[noun] the idea that people, like flowers, bloom in their own time and individual ways

In this meadow
where the earth
breathes free,
a tapestry of life
unfurls
with grace.
Each stem,
each petal,
a testament to time,
a silent witness
to the sun's
embrace.

Here,
the flowers
bloom
in their own way,
in their own time,
with colors bright
or pale,
Some rise early,

flowering

eager
for the dawn,
Others wait,
patient
beneath the veil.

The dandelions,
first to greet
the light,
Their golden heads
nodding
in the breeze,
Whisper
of the morning's
gentle touch,
a quiet promise
carried through the trees.

Each bloom is
different,
yet
none compete,
For in this field,
there's space for every kind,
The daisies
spread
their snowy petals
wide,
While violets hide,

content
to stay behind.

The sunflowers turn,
majestic
bold
and tall,
following
the sun's arc
through the sky,
their faces bright
with warmth
and golden hues,
Reaching high,
as if they
long
to fly.

And then
the poppies,
fiery and intense,
Emerge
in bursts of red
amid the green.
They blaze
with passion,
fleeting
but profound,
a beauty

flowering

in the briefness
of their sheen.

The lupines stand,
a sturdy,
quiet force,
their purple spires
a beacon
in the wind.
They bloom in clusters,
strong
and intertwined,
a testament to unity
within.

Among them all,
the humble dandelion,
Soft and fragile,
yet
resilient too,
It blooms with grace,
then scatters to the wind,
Its seeds
a dance of life,
both old and new.

Each flower
has its moment in the sun,
Its time to shine,

oubaitori

to grow,
to fade,
to fall,
and
in this meadow,
none
are left behind,
For every petal
plays a vital role.

The wind moves gently
through the swaying grass,
A breath
of life that carries
whispered dreams.
The flowers bend,
but never break or bow;
they know their
time,
and trust
in nature's schemes.

And as I walk among
this living field,
I see the
truth
in every leaf
and every stem:
that life is not meant to follow

flowering

just one path,
But many roads that
lead
to where
we
are meant to go.

The roses bloom
with thorns
that guard their
hearts,
their petals soft,
yet
layered with intent,
while
wildflowers
weave a different tale,
of freedom
found in places heaven-sent.

The orchids,
rare,
await their perfect time,
To burst in bloom
with colours
rich and deep,
They know
the value of the patient wait,

oubaitori

Their beauty
lies in promises
they keep.

The daffodils
that trumpet in the spring,
With heads held high,
proclaim
their time has come.
They light the way
for those who follow
close,
a guide
for those who
seek
the morning sun.

In this meadow,
where each flower thrives,
no two are the same,
yet all belong
as one,
their roots
entwined
beneath the fertile soil.
Their lives
a dance,
a song that's never done.

flowering

And when the sun dips
low
to kiss the earth,
the flowers close, but
not in fear or dread,
for they have bloomed,
and will again in time,
Their beauty
found in every hue
they've shed.

Each bloom a story,
each a verse of life
a chapter
in the meadow's endless tome.
They blossom, fade,
and scatter to the wind,
Yet leave behind a memory,
a home.

So let them grow,
in their own time
and in their own way,
for in their difference
lies the meadow's charm.
No flower rushed,
no bloom cut short or swayed;
all find their place within

oubaitori

this world,
this calm.

And in this meadow,
wild
and free
and true,
there's room for all,
no need for rush or race,
for every flower knows
just when to bloom,
and in its time,
will find its
rightful place.

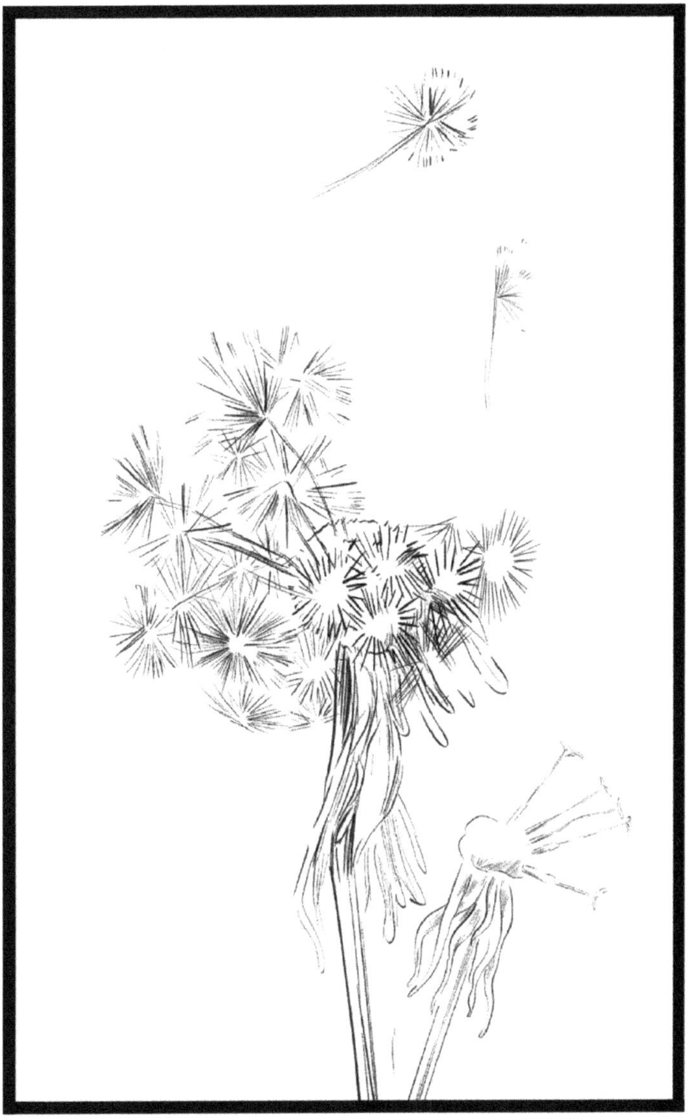

wabi sabi

[adjective] Finding beauty in imperfection, impermanence, or simplicity

As I stand in this field of dandelions,
Swaying their heads to a distant melody,
I sway with them,
one with the simple harmony of life.

As I run my hands through these dandelions,
Soft and comforting as cotton,
I smile with them,
one with the simple harmony of life.

As I wish upon these dandelions,
wistful, fantastical and wild as the heart of nature,
I blow at them gently,
one with the simple harmony of life.

As I watch them leave, those beautiful dandelions,
swirling up into the world and drifting away,
I wave my hand in goodbye to a short-lived, pure, beauty,
one with the simple harmony of life.

epilogue

In the quiet of the morning, as the world awakens,
I sit with the stillness, a companion now,
The cup of tea warm in my hands,
Its steam a gentle whisper of comfort.

I breathe in the calm of this simple moment,
No rush, no need to chase or grasp,
For I have learned the art of being here,
In this place, with this self, just as it is.

The light filters softly through the window,
Casting shadows that dance upon the walls,
Each one a reminder of the beauty found
In the spaces between, in the imperfection.

The scars I carry, once so heavy and dark,
Are lighter now, softened by time and grace,
They are part of my story, woven into the fabric
Of who I am, and who I've become.

In the quiet unfolding of this morning light,
I see now that life is a flowering,
Each moment a petal, each breath a bloom,
Opening in its own time, in its own way.

epilogue

The journey has been long, and not without pain,
But here, in this soft and gentle dawn,
I find a peace I never knew was possible,
A peace that comes from within, from accepting.

I am here, in this moment, in this life,
And it is enough, more than enough.
The world outside continues to turn,
but I am content to simply be:

Here, in this quiet, perfect imperfection.

flowering.

conclusion

As the final pages of *flowering* come to a close, I find myself reflecting on the journey that both you, the reader, and I, as the writer, have taken through these verses. The poems in this collection are more than just words on a page; they are markers of a path—a path that winds through the valleys of pain, climbs the mountains of realization, and finds rest in the quiet meadows of acceptance. This journey has been one of growth and transformation, a testament to the resilience of the human spirit and the beauty that emerges from embracing both our light and our shadows.

The metaphor of *flowering* has woven itself throughout these poems, not merely as a symbol of growth, but as a reflection of the complex, often contradictory nature of life itself. Flowers, in their transient beauty, remind us that everything in life is temporary—yet in this impermanence, we find meaning. The blooming of a flower is a momentary burst of life, vibrant and full, before it inevitably fades. And yet, it is this very cycle of growth, bloom, and decay that enriches the soil, making way for new life to emerge. This collection has sought to capture this cycle, to explore the moments of beauty, pain, love, and loss that define our existence, and to celebrate the journey of becoming.

conclusion

In writing *flowering,* I wanted to explore the idea that growth is not linear, nor is it always visible to the eye. Just as a seed takes root in the darkness of the earth, so too do we often grow in the unseen corners of our lives, where light has yet to reach. These poems reflect the varied and often unpredictable ways in which we evolve, each one a testament to the unique paths we all take in our own *flowering.* Some flowers bloom in the spring, others in the summer, and still others in the quiet of autumn. Each has its time, and each brings its own beauty to the world.

The concept of *oubaitori,* the idea that people, like flowers, bloom in their own time and in their own way, has been a guiding principle throughout this collection. It is a reminder that we are not in competition with one another, but rather, we each have our own journey to follow, our own seasons of growth. This collection invites you to honour your own path, to recognize the beauty in your unique experiences, and to trust in the timing of your life. There is no rush, no race to the finish; there is only the unfolding of your own story, petal by petal.

As you have journeyed through these poems, you may have recognized echoes of your own life within the lines. Perhaps a verse or a stanza resonated with a particular moment in your past, or maybe it illuminated something within you that you had not yet put into words. Poetry has a way of reaching into the depths of our souls, of touching the parts of us that are often hidden from the light. It is my hope that *flowering* has offered you a space to reflect,

conclusion

to heal, and to grow. That these poems have been more than just words on a page, but companions on your own journey of becoming.

The final poem, *wabi sabi,* serves as both an end and a beginning—a recognition of the beauty found in imperfection, in the fleeting nature of life, and in the simplicity of the present moment. It is a reminder that life is not about striving for perfection, but about embracing the imperfections that make us human. It is in the cracks, the flaws, and the imperfections that the light gets in, and it is in these places that we find our true selves. *wabi sabi* is the culmination of the journey, the *flowering* of the soul that has come to accept itself fully, with all its beauty and its scars.

As you close this book, I invite you to carry with you the lessons of *flowering*. To remember that growth is a process, not a destination. That every moment, whether painful or joyous, is a part of your own unique *flowering*. That you are a part of this vast, interconnected tapestry of life, and that your bloom, whenever and however it may come, is an essential thread in the fabric of existence.

Thank you for allowing these poems to be a part of your journey. May you continue to bloom in your own time, in your own way, and may you find peace in the knowledge that you are exactly where you are meant to be.

In the end, the act of *flowering* is not about reaching a final form, but about the ongoing process of becoming.

conclusion

It is about embracing the present moment, with all its imperfections and possibilities, and allowing yourself to grow, to change, and to bloom in the way that only you can. This is the essence of *flowering*—the recognition that life is a continuous journey of growth and transformation, and that each of us is a flower, unfolding in our own time, in our own way.

May your journey be rich with beauty, love, and light, and may you find joy in the simple act of *flowering*.

poet's notes

sunrise

sunrise serves as the opening poem of the collection, symbolizing the beginning of both a new day and the journey of emotional and spiritual growth. The poem uses the natural phenomenon of sunrise as a metaphor for renewal, hope, and the start of a transformative process. Just as the sun rises gradually, bringing light to the world, the speaker experiences the slow unfolding of life, joy, and new possibilities.

The structure of the poem mirrors the slow, deliberate nature of a sunrise. The lines grow in length and intensity as the poem progresses, reflecting the gradual spread of light across the sky.

This poem's simplicity and brevity serve as a symbolic dawn for the rest of the collection, suggesting that with every sunrise comes the potential for new experiences, emotions, and growth. It introduces the central theme of the collection: the ongoing process of becoming, much like the sun rises each day to cast light on the world.

selcouth

selcouth—meaning unfamiliar, rare, and strange—captures the wonder and strangeness that accompany new experiences. The poem uses the aurora borealis as a metaphor for encountering something beautiful yet unfamiliar. The aurora's flashing lights, weaving through the sky in bursts of color— "They flash red and blue and green," and "They play and fight and clash"—mirror the unpredictable nature of new emotional or intellectual discoveries.

The language reflects the simultaneous awe and confusion that often arise during these moments of discovery. Descriptors like "strange and peculiar and haunting" emphasize the wonder and discomfort that come with encountering the unknown. The aurora symbolizes the beauty in navigating new experiences that are mesmerizing yet challenging, much like moments of personal growth.

poet's notes

The poem's short, repetitive lines mirror the rhythmic bursts of the aurora, building intensity and heightening the sense of mystery and power associated with the northern lights. The structure echoes the unpredictable flashes of light, just as new experiences often unfold in unexpected ways.

Ultimately, selcouth celebrates the beauty of the unfamiliar. It invites readers to embrace the unknown and appreciate the rare and unpredictable moments in life, reflecting the emotional journey of venturing into uncharted territory where wonder intertwines with strangeness.

kalopsia

kalopsia delves into the concept of seeing something as more beautiful than it truly is, using the mythical figure of the siren as a metaphor for illusion, desire, and deception. The poem captures the allure of the siren—seemingly perfect and irresistible—and how those who fall under her spell are drawn in by a false sense of beauty, only to be destroyed by the reality hidden beneath the surface.

The imagery in the first half of the poem paints a picture of a captivating and enchanting figure: "scales glitter and reflect secrets of the sea," "hair of the sun," and "skin of snow." These descriptions evoke a sense of ethereal, almost untouchable beauty, with the siren acting as a mesmerizing force who sings to the desires of those who encounter her. Her voice, echoing repeatedly, symbolizes the seductive pull that entrances sailors and pulls them into her orbit.

However, as the poem progresses, the tone shifts. The once-perfect image begins to unravel, revealing a far darker truth beneath the surface. The siren's beauty and allure are a façade for something much more dangerous. "Can you not see claws beneath porcelain-plain gloves?" and "glistening fangs beneath cherry full lips" introduce the idea that what appears beautiful can also be deadly. This shift in tone reflects the poem's exploration of the tension between idealization and reality, as those who are mesmerized by the siren's outward appearance fail to see the danger lying in wait.

The poem's structure also mirrors this gradual unraveling of illusion. The first half of the poem features fluid, long lines that flow like the siren's song, capturing the hypnotic allure of kalopsia. But as the truth of her nature is revealed, the lines become shorter and more abrupt, with sharp imagery that breaks the trance-like rhythm, echoing the sharpness of her claws and fangs.

The repeated warnings from the lone sailor who stands apart from the others serve as a counterpoint to the illusion of beauty. His refusal to be swayed by the siren's enchantments is symbolic of seeing through false promises, of recognizing the dangerous reality behind the illusion. His words—"Do not lose your melodies of truth"—are a call to resist the allure of deception and stay grounded in reality.

The poem ends in tragedy, as the sailors who were seduced by the siren's song are dragged down into darkness, a metaphor for being consumed by illusion. The siren's true nature is fully revealed as she "slits with her now-revealed claws," and the disillusionment is complete. The contrast between the beauty promised by the siren and the death she delivers serves as a cautionary tale about the dangers of believing in idealized or deceptive appearances.

kalopsia ultimately reflects the human tendency to idealize and romanticize, warning that what we see as beautiful and perfect may, in fact, be an illusion masking something far darker. The siren embodies this concept, serving as both a figure of desire and a harbinger of destruction.

parasite

parasite explores the insidious nature of toxic relationships through the metaphor of a vine strangling a sapling. The vine, initially a symbol of companionship and shared goals, slowly tightens its hold, revealing its true parasitic nature. The sapling, too naive to foresee the danger, is gradually suffocated, reflecting how such relationships often begin symbiotically but become harmful over time.

The poem's structure mirrors this progression: long, flowing lines give way to shorter, constricted phrases as the parasite's grip tightens. Words like "coil," "clenches," and "gripped" evoke the increasing suffocation of the sapling, symbolizing the loss of freedom and vitality.

By the final stanza, the sapling "flopped, tumbling into its losing void," representing the complete depletion of the host, while the parasite—now victorious—moves on to find its next victim. parasite serves as a cautionary tale, highlighting how seemingly promising relationships can become destructive, leaving the host powerless and drained.

poet's notes

agowilt

agowilt captures the overwhelming and uncontrollable nature of sudden fear through fragmented, urgent language. The poem is structured to mimic the physical and emotional experience of a panic attack, using short, abrupt sentences and repetition to convey the sensation of losing control. The speaker's voice becomes increasingly desperate, reflecting the spiraling effect of fear that consumes both mind and body.

The use of natural imagery—thunder, earth, and air—intensifies the experience of fear, creating a sense that the world itself is turning against the speaker. These elements act as external manifestations of the internal chaos, heightening the sense of disorientation and helplessness. The poem's pacing quickens as the fear becomes more intense, with phrases like "I can't think. I can't breathe," and "Help me, I'm scared" emphasizing the frantic urgency of the speaker's thoughts.

The repetition of "please" in the final lines conveys a desperate plea for relief, as the speaker is overwhelmed by fear. agowilt offers a raw and visceral portrayal of panic, reflecting the uncontrollable nature of such emotions through its disjointed form and intense imagery.

douleur

douleur is a French word meaning misery, anguish, and excruciating pain. The poem vividly depicts the overwhelming nature of suffering through the metaphor of a tidal wave, which symbolizes the uncontrollable force of emotional and physical torment. The ocean imagery emphasizes the inevitability and destructiveness of pain, as it "ravenously consumed everything in sight till all that was, was entombed."

The third stanza is a list of intense, sharp descriptors—each representing a different facet of anguish—where the first letter of each word spells out "unbearable" vertically. This acrostic detail underscores the thematic focus of the poem: the unendurable nature of profound suffering.

The final word, "HURT," stands alone as a powerful exclamation point, summarizing the totality of the pain described throughout the poem. douleur captures the relentless, crushing weight of anguish through both its imagery and form, conveying the multifaceted and consuming aspects of misery.

poet's notes

rancour

rancour is a fierce expression of deep-seated resentment and all-consuming anger, represented by a raging forest fire. The poem serves as the emotional climax of the pain experienced in earlier poems like douleur (hurt) and parasite (betrayal). The fire metaphor reflects the uncontrollable and destructive nature of anger, burning through everything in its path.

The repeated phrase "Burn and burn" emphasizes the relentless and cyclical nature of hatred, as it consumes both the object of the anger and the person who harbours it. Each stanza introduces increasingly violent imagery—"Devour and eradicate," "Growl and snarl and ravage and shred"—showcasing the escalation of fury, as the speaker seeks total annihilation of what has wronged them.

The rhythmic repetition in the poem mimics the relentless spreading of a wildfire, while words like "roar" and "hiss" give the fire a voice, personifying anger as a force that cannot be tamed. This poem is the embodiment of unchecked rage, reflecting how the pain of betrayal (parasite and kalopsia) fuels an inferno that demands destruction. rancour conveys the vicious cycle of anger, perpetuating itself until nothing is left standing.

lacuna

lacuna captures the hollow emptiness that follows an intense emotional release, representing the blank space left behind after the anger and destruction of rancour. The title, which refers to a missing part or blank space, reflects the emotional void the speaker experiences—where once there was pain, now there is only exhaustion and silence.

The poem's repetitive structure—"I whisper to myself in the silence"—reinforces the sense of isolation and emptiness, as if the speaker is left alone to confront the aftermath of their emotional storm. Each stanza presents images of depletion: "When rain is lost," "rivers are sand," and "the emptiness is inescapable." These natural metaphors emphasize a sense of lifelessness and barrenness, where everything once vital has been drained away.

The poem's rhythm slows, matching the speaker's exhaustion, as the vivid emotions from earlier poems have been spent. lacuna symbolizes the quiet, numbing void that follows a cathartic release of emotion. It is the moment where there is nothing left to feel, and the speaker is left to face the silence and the stillness, having emptied themselves of everything.

petrichor

petrichor reflects on the deep loneliness that lingers after moments of connection are lost, using the metaphor of the earth after a rainfall. The scent of petrichor symbolizes the bittersweet memory of companionship, just as the earth holds onto the scent of rain long after it has passed. This poem is a meditation on solitude, where even nature experiences the ache of separation.

The structure of the poem mirrors this sense of isolation. The short, deliberate lines and frequent line breaks create pauses that allow the reader to feel the quiet and stillness that follows the rain. The subdued imagery—"the sky had wept softly," "a quiet drizzle on parched ground"—creates a sense of emptiness and longing. The earth's "thirsty soil" reflects the speaker's emotional hunger, which is quickly satisfied but leaves behind an even deeper void when the rain is gone.

The repetition of words like "quiet" and "silence" reinforces the theme of loneliness, while the closing lines shift to an almost mournful tone, with the earth "left to dry and die." The scent of petrichor becomes a metaphor for the lingering memory of connection that can no longer be reclaimed, deepening the feeling of loneliness that permeates the poem.

desvelado

desvelado (Spanish for 'sleepless') conveys the quiet, reflective solitude that comes with sleeplessness. The poem uses the imagery of a serene, moonlit night to represent personal introspection, where the silence of the world mirrors the speaker's internal stillness. The poem's setting—a deserted shore under a cold, distant moon—emphasizes the sense of isolation, yet it is not harsh. Instead, it allows space for reflection.

The repetitive imagery of the "cold distant moon" underscores the stillness of the night, while elements like the "thin, cold mist" and "shadows of sparse foliage" reflect the speaker's inner thoughts shifting gently through the quiet. The subtle transition from night to the hopeful appearance of "a single, faint star" serves as a metaphor for the gradual emergence of hope, no matter how distant or faint it may seem.

poet's notes

The poem's structure, with its slow, measured pace and short lines, enhances the contemplative mood. The repetition of soft sounds and gentle movements creates a lull, inviting the reader to experience the same calm. In its final lines, desvelado hints at the possibility of fulfilment, as the "quiet of the night spoke softly of hope," suggesting that peace and clarity may follow moments of quiet reflection.

komorebi

komorebi captures the beauty of sunlight filtering through the trees, symbolizing the arrival of hope after darkness. The title, a Japanese word that refers to the interplay of sunlight through leaves, evokes the feeling of light breaking through the shadows—just as hope can gently emerge in moments of despair.

The imagery of the forest waking up, with leaves "whispering prophecies" and "soft beams of light" dancing on the forest floor, reflects a sense of renewal and possibility. The poem's use of light as a central metaphor conveys the quiet arrival of hope, tender and gradual, as it transforms the darkness of night into golden warmth. The morning dew, turning sunlight into rainbows, further emphasizes the idea that even the smallest moments can refract light and joy into the world.

The structure is gentle and flowing, mimicking the movement of sunlight and the soft rustle of leaves. The final image of a "golden ribbon of light" winding through the woods suggests a path forward, guiding the reader toward a future illuminated with hope and possibility. komorebi reminds us that light, like hope, often arrives quietly but transforms the world with its presence.

apricity

apricity is a celebration of first love, expressed through the metaphor of winter's warmth—the gentle, golden light of the sun breaking through the cold. The title, meaning the warmth of the sun in winter, reflects how love, even in the coldest and most still moments, brings life, warmth, and hope. The imagery in the poem creates a tender and delicate contrast between the frozen world and the gentle heat of a new, blossoming love.

The natural setting of winter, with frost, snow, and bare branches, acts as a canvas upon which love paints its warmth. The poem's extended imagery—sunlight softening icicles, morning dew reflecting rainbows, and the snow shimmering

poet's notes

under the light—conveys how love transforms and illuminates even the coldest of landscapes. The frozen river, described as stirring beneath its surface, symbolizes the awakening of emotions and possibility that first love brings.

The structure of the poem mirrors the feeling of first love: soft and flowing, with long lines that move like a gentle breeze through a wintery world. The repeated references to warmth, light, and touch emphasize the physical and emotional comfort that love provides, even in an environment traditionally associated with cold and isolation.

Throughout the poem, there is a steady interplay between cold and warmth, night and day, suggesting that first love exists in harmony with both. The light of love doesn't overpower the darkness of winter but works alongside it, creating a balance that is both comforting and enduring. The love described in apricity is tender yet strong, able to endure the "cold wolf" of winter and the "unsheathed claws" of darkness.

The poem concludes by emphasizing the steadfast nature of this first love—a warmth that "refused to fade" and turned even the darkest night into a sanctuary. It highlights the idea that love, like the sun in winter, is both gentle and constant, capable of transforming the world and making even the coldest moments feel alive.

sillage

sillage explores the inevitable and necessary grief that follows the end of a first love, using the metaphor of autumn's fading beauty to reflect the lingering presence of something once cherished. The title, meaning the scent that lingers after someone or something has gone, evokes the sense of loss that remains even after love has passed. The poem's villanelle form—with its repeating lines—mirrors the cyclical nature of grief and the persistent memories that refuse to fade.

Autumn's imagery plays a central role, with "golden remnants of summer" and "brittle leaves" symbolizing the remnants of love that are still felt even after it has decayed. The repeated phrase "The leaves descend gently in autumn's whispered hush" captures the soft, inevitable fading of passion, while the "fleeting, fragrant ghost" refers to the intangible yet persistent memories of the past.

poet's notes

The poem's melancholic tone is enhanced by the imagery of a "mournful wind" and "bare branches," suggesting that while love may be gone, its impression remains. sillage captures the bittersweet nature of parting with first love—necessary for growth, yet leaving behind a tender, haunting imprint.

cicatrize

cicatrize reflects on the idea that scars, whether physical or emotional, are necessary for healing and growth. Using the metaphor of an ancient oak tree damaged by a storm, the poem explores how even deep wounds can give rise to newfound strength and beauty. The scar on the oak, rather than symbolizing weakness or loss, becomes a mark of resilience and renewal.

The oak tree represents endurance, standing tall despite the storm's destructive force. The imagery of sap flowing from the wound and new leaves unfurling symbolizes the natural process of healing, as life continues to emerge from even the most painful experiences. The repeated references to scars as "sacred seams" and "silvered lines" highlight the transformation of pain into something meaningful and purposeful.

The poem emphasizes that healing comes not from external forces but from within. Time, patience, and nature's steady rhythm are the true remedies, and the oak's scars serve as reminders of what was endured and overcome. cicatrize ultimately celebrates the idea that everything—pain, loss, and struggle—has a purpose, and that scars are not marks of defeat but emblems of survival, strength, and renewal.

metanoia

metanoia is a vivid exploration of personal transformation, using the life cycle of a butterfly as a metaphor for profound change in the mind, heart, and self. The poem follows the butterfly's journey from a caterpillar, through the stages of metamorphosis, to the moment of emergence as a fully formed, iridescent being. This natural process symbolizes the internal transformation that comes from perseverance, growth, and self-discovery.

The progression of the poem mirrors the stages of transformation—beginning with struggle and uncertainty as the caterpillar pushes through "oozy slime" toward a distant goal. The leaf symbolizes the promise of

poet's notes

change, something soft and full of life, which nourishes the protagonist and begins the transformation.

The cocoon, described as a place of "peaceful comfort," represents introspection, where the speaker waits patiently for the right moment to emerge. The shift in the body—wings forming, weightlessness—is the embodiment of change taking place, both physically and emotionally.

The final stanzas celebrate the butterfly's rebirth, as it breaks free from the cocoon, fully transformed into a creature of strength and beauty. metanoia emphasizes the power of transformation, where struggle gives way to glory and self-realization, symbolized by the butterfly soaring into the sky.

koi no yokan

koi no yokan captures the quiet certainty and inevitability of falling in love from the moment two souls first meet. The poem is written in terza rima, a form known for its interlocking rhymes (ABA BCB CDC), which mirrors the natural, inevitable pull of two people toward each other. Using the imagery of the ocean and shore, the poem symbolizes the delicate but powerful pull of love, as natural and unstoppable as the tides. The title, a Japanese phrase meaning the premonition of falling in love upon first meeting, sets the tone for the gentle and rhythmic interplay between the sea and the shore.

The waves, representing love, steadily approach the shore, symbolizing the heart that is ready to receive. The ocean's "tender touch" on the waiting sand evokes the inevitability of connection, as both the sea and shore are drawn to one another without hesitation or fear. The poem's flowing tercets mirror the graceful rhythm of the ocean, reflecting how love naturally unfolds over time.

The final lines, "The tides will rise—I welcome you, my love," solidify the acceptance of this inevitable connection, where love is met without resistance. koi no yokan expresses the beauty of knowing that, like the meeting of sea and shore, love is destined to intertwine, creating a sense of peace and fulfilment.

querencia

querencia explores the concept of finding one's true home—a place of safety, where strength is drawn and one's authentic self is fully embraced. The poem is set in a secluded cove, symbolizing a personal sanctuary where the speaker finds peace, comfort, and a deep connection with the natural world. The word querencia refers to a place where one feels most at home, and the poem reflects this sense of belonging and contentment.

Written in ottava rima, a form known for its elegant structure and flowing rhythm, the poem mirrors the gentle ebb and flow of the ocean, which is central to the imagery. The recurring themes of the sea's embrace, the moonlit waves, and the glowing walls of the cove evoke a sense of tranquillity and timelessness, where the speaker feels completely at ease.

The cove, described as a place where "earth and ocean meet," represents the union of opposites—solid and fluid, strength and tenderness. The imagery of waves gently kissing the shore and the ocean's lullaby reinforces the idea of a safe, nurturing space that fosters authenticity and inner strength.

The final stanzas emphasize the dissolution of time and boundaries within the cove, where the speaker is no longer searching or yearning, but instead feels whole and complete. The poem captures the serenity of finding a place where one belongs, where both the external and internal worlds align, creating a sense of profound peace and fulfilment.

raison d'être

raison d'être explores the concept of purpose and existence, using the sun as the central metaphor to convey life's meaning and the sustaining force behind all creation. The poem presents the sun as a powerful, unwavering source of life and energy, symbolizing the constant light that guides the world through cycles of time, growth, and renewal. The sun's steady rise and fall serve as a metaphor for the purpose that gives form and direction to everything in the universe.

Written in heroic couplets (pairs of rhyming lines in iambic pentameter), the poem reflects the sun's steady rhythm and unending presence. The progression of the day—from dawn to zenith, sunset to night—mirrors the process of finding one's purpose in life, which unfolds gradually but powerfully.

Each stanza reflects how the sun affects different aspects of the natural world— mountains, oceans, creatures, and seasons—showing that every part of life is connected to the sun's light. This reinforces the idea that the sun, much like a personal sense of purpose, touches everything and is a guiding force for all that exists.

poet's notes

The poem culminates in the understanding that, just as the sun rises unfailingly, our purpose endures, guiding us through the challenges and changes of life. The sun's constancy becomes a symbol of the clarity and strength we derive from our own purpose, illuminating the world and sustaining life as it rises and falls without fail.

oubaitori

oubaitori is a meditation on the natural process of growth and self-realization, reflecting the understanding that every person, like a flower, blooms in their own time and in their own way. The poem draws on the imagery of a diverse meadow, where each flower represents a different path, a unique pace, and a distinct expression of life.

The metaphor of blooming flowers—dandelions, daisies, sunflowers, and poppies, among others—symbolizes the idea that no two lives unfold in the same manner. Each flower thrives in its own time, from the early bloomers like the dandelion to the rare and patient orchids, emphasizing the theme of individual growth. The sun's role as a constant presence mirrors the forces in life that nurture and guide us, while the flowers represent how we respond to these influences.

The free verse structure of the poem allows for a flowing, natural rhythm, reflecting the gentle and unhurried unfolding of life. The poem's tone is one of calm assurance, conveying the message that there is no need to rush or compare one's path to another's.

The final stanzas reinforce that all flowers—and by extension, all people—have their time to shine, and none are left behind. oubaitori teaches that growth, like nature, is organic and unique to each individual, and it celebrates the beauty of blooming in one's own time, trusting in the natural rhythm of life.

wabi sabi

wabi sabi reflects the acceptance of imperfection, impermanence, and simplicity, celebrating the quiet beauty found in life's fleeting moments. The poem, with its imagery of dandelions, serves as a metaphor for the speaker's final stage of healing—finding peace with life's transience and embracing the joy in small, simple things. The dandelions, both delicate and ephemeral, symbolize the fragile, fleeting nature of life, while their drifting seeds represent the release of past burdens and the gentle acceptance of change.

The repetition of "one with the simple harmony of life" creates a meditative rhythm, mirroring the speaker's alignment with the natural flow of life. This phrase emphasizes the unity between the speaker and nature, illustrating a profound acceptance of life's imperfections. The act of blowing dandelions, often associated with wishes and letting go, reflects the speaker's newfound peace—able to smile, appreciate, and release, fully healed from past wounds.

The free verse form allows the poem to flow naturally, echoing the theme of impermanence and the effortless grace of being at peace with one's humanity. wabi sabi encapsulates the beauty of imperfection and impermanence, offering a quiet, reflective conclusion to the collection, where the speaker has found contentment and healing, fully in tune with life's gentle, ever-changing rhythm.

with gratitude

First and foremost, I would like to express my deepest gratitude to my family for their endless patience, love, and belief in me. No development of my own, in my life or in my writing, could have been possible without the combined influence and growth fostered by my family. Thank you for choosing me everyday, and for always being there for me when I needed you most. Thank you for taking me to beautiful places, and for raising me to always be in relentless pursuit of improvement and growth. Your constant encouragement has been the bedrock upon which I've built this work.

Daddy, thank you for your honest feedback and constructive criticism, which have helped me work on myself and my projects. Your dependability is unshakable, and I owe you my love for reading. I cherish all your goodnight stories about *Eragon* and *Saphira*. I'm proud to be Papa's Pari.

Madre, thank you for listening to me and for trying your best in everything you do; your efforts never go unnoticed. You've always been my source of quiet strength. Thank you both for supporting my dreams, even when they seemed intangible.

To my older brother Pranay, you old porcupine, thank you for making every day entertaining, and for paving a path for

with gratitude

me to follow. I'll make sure my first purchase is that dosa from our favorite place at Teen Batti.

To my grandfather, thank you for being an overflowing well of love, attention, advice, and truth.

To my cousins, Annie, Soham, Satu and Ruhani—thank you for being more like real siblings than cousins. Your love and unwavering support have brightened my life immeasurably. I can't wait to continue travelling the world with you, making memories, and creating new stories to share.

To my friends—Laila, Navya, Ayu, Nyah, Shania, Mehek, Antara, Aarav, Siddh, Darsh, Navi, and all those who have walked with me on this path—thank you for offering both comfort and distraction when I was needed it most. Your companionship has been a constant, and your unwavering belief in my creative journey has meant the world to me. Lai and Navya, especially, thank you for standing by my side through the years, and for reading every single draft of every unfinished novel idea. You've been with me from the beginning, and I'm forever grateful.

To Zara, my dear illustrator and oldest friend, I think we were truly fortunate to find each other. The countless things we've done together and the ways we've grown together seem infinite. From organizing charity concerts to creating magazines, we've conquered every feat hand in hand—me, the writer, and you, the artist. By some stroke of fortune, we've found the perfect counterpart in each other. Thank you for being such a wonderful human and friend throughout all 17 years of my life. We've climbed mountains together. Though university will part us physically, I hope you continue scaling even greater ranges on your own. I'll always be there with you in spirit, just as you'll be with me. I look forward to our future projects, for I'm certain that the best is yet to come.

Ms. Ipshita, whose guidance and encouragement through the years have been instrumental in shaping this collection—thank you for your unwavering support. From reading the most bizarre stories since I was 10, to still greeting me with the brightest smile, you have been a constant in my life, and the catalyst for my writing ambitions. You were my first mentor, and will remain so for the rest of my life.

Ms. Martins, whose classroom was an environment that nurtured imagination, thank you for teaching me how much beauty writing can hold. I still remember that assignment—*I Have a Dream*—where every letter of the title started a successive line of a poem. I wrote about my love for reading and how it transports you to worlds unheard of, where anything is possible. That lesson became embedded in my mind, and I've carried it with me ever since. You taught me how to dream.

Ms. Gupta, whose unexpected and utterly extraordinary blind faith opened doors to me with unending corridors that I never thought could be mine to explore, thank you for trusting in me. Thank you for daring me to take a risk, to take a plunge for something I believe in strongly. Your kindness, your genuine care, and your love, are things I am incredibly grateful for. Working under you, I learned that the writing in my little notebook does not have to stay there. You taught me that I have a voice, and that there are people who would want to listen to it.

Mr. Thapa, whose current tutelage has instilled confidence in both myself and my passions—thank you for your insights and your steadfast guidance. You have not only improved my writing, but deepened my understanding of poetry as an art form. Your encouragement has taught me to work harder towards accomplishing my goals.

Dr. Parmar, whose unwavering support and constant encouragement have meant the world to me. Your kindness and open-mindedness, whether promoting *Soundwave* or considering our magazine proposal, have always made me feel valued as both a student and a writer. I am deeply honoured that you agreed to write the foreword to *flowering*, and I am grateful for your dedication to fostering student growth and creativity. Your guidance has been truly inspiring, and I feel fortunate to have learned from you.

Finally, to you, the readers, who will bring your own experiences to these pages—thank you. Your presence on this journey is deeply appreciated, and I am honoured to share this work with you. I hope these words resonate with you and remind you that you are your own home, a place worthy of protection and love.

author bio

Advita Mundhra is a 17-year-old poet and writer from Mumbai, India, whose love for words has shaped her journey from a young age. Her debut poetry collection is a delicate exploration of growth, healing, and transformation, using nature as a powerful metaphor for the human experience. Her work has been featured in The Cathedralite, where she served as Head Editor for its first student-run edition, guiding the magazine to capture the voices and creativity of her peers.

Deeply passionate about both literature and music, Advita finds inspiration in a wide range of artistic influences—from the magical worlds of Harry Potter and Christopher Paolini's Inheritance Cycle, to the emotional depth of musicals like The Phantom of the Opera and Hamilton. Music plays an essential role in her life, and she draws from the likes of

author bio

Whitney Houston, Celine Dion, and Bruno Mars to fuel her creative spirit.

When she's not writing or lost in a bookshop, you can find Advita enjoying a bowl of ramen or sipping a cup of steaming oat-milk coffee, wrapped in a thick blanket, soaking in the beauty of a well-loved novel. With a deep appreciation for self-expression and storytelling, she hopes her poetry resonates with readers, guiding them through their own journeys of reflection and self-discovery.

Milton Keynes UK
Ingram Content Group UK Ltd.
UKHW041833121124
451129UK00006B/55